THE CONCEPT OF
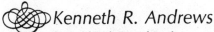
CORPORATE
STRATEGY

Kenneth R. Andrews

*Donald Kirk David Professor
of Business Administration
Harvard University*

1980   Revised Edition

RICHARD D. IRWIN, INC.   Homewood, Illinois   60430

ISBN 0-256-02371-9 (paperbound)

ISBN 0-87094-208-5 (hardbound)

Library of Congress Catalog No. 79–56086

Printed in the United States of America

7 8 9 0 K 7 6 5

# Preface

This revision of *The Concept of Corporate Strategy*, originally published in 1971, acknowledges the impact of the last nine years on business education and corporate experience in strategic planning. Because attention to strategic issues is now so common as to constitute a verbal fad, I have shortened the argument, refined definitions, modernized examples, and shifted the emphasis from exhortation to embodiment as an organization process. The central idea remains intact. The highest function of the executive is still seen as leading the continuous process of determining the nature of the enterprise and setting, revising, and achieving its goals.

The substance of this book is the subject matter of the field of professional study usually called *business policy*. It has appeared in *Business Policy: Text and Cases*, published first by Richard D. Irwin, Inc., in 1965, with Edmund P. Learned, C. Roland Christensen, William D. Guth, and myself as authors. That volume currently appears in its fourth edition with Christensen, Joseph L. Bower, and myself as authors; the fifth edition will appear soon. The combination of text and company cases is widely used in graduate business schools and programs

of executive education. This version of the text is issued
for use by executive readers who will consider it against
the opportunities of their own companies. It becomes
available to students for use with cases different from the
selection we offer. These may be assembled in many
combinations from the hundreds available from the Intercollegiate Case Clearing House.

Business policy is the study of the functions and responsibilities of the senior management in a company,
the crucial problems that affect the success of the total
enterprise, and the decisions that determine its direction,
shape its future, and produce the results desired. The policy problems of business, like those of policy in public
affairs, have to do with the choice of purposes, the mold-
ing of organization identity and character, the unending
definition of what needs to be done, and the mobilization
of resources for the attainment of goals in the face of aggressive competition or adverse circumstance.

The concept of strategy originated in professional
schools of management. It has developed during the last
20 years out of a long effort to perfect an integrative cap-
stone course in the M.B.A. curriculum—one devoted to
the problems of the company *as a whole* as seen from the
perspective of the president or chief executive. Its format
has traditionally included complex cases, continually re-
newed, which present as far as practicable the total situation of a company. Students are asked to analyze the state
of the company, to identify the principal problems in its
situation, and to prescribe a program of action. They soon
discover that only the determination of suitable objectives makes possible a satisfactorily rational choice
among action alternatives. The discussion of individual
companies therefore matures into a consideration of how
to formulate an appropriate pattern of purpose and policy
and how to convert plans into results.

The knowledge, skills, and attitudes developed in such study comprise the professional orientation of the generalist who can apply analytical intelligence, entrepreneurial imagination, and administrative ability to opportunity.

The business policy course, required of M.B.A. students for decades—at Harvard and at many other universities—has in many variations often comprised the core course of university and company executive programs. At Harvard in particular, where the M.B.A. program is directed to the practice of management rather than to the mastery of one or more related academic disciplines, courses in marketing, production, and control, for example, culminate often in consideration of strategic issues.

Through the influence of M.B.A. graduates, especially those entering consulting firms newly established or diversified to conduct a practice in strategic planning, the long-standing natural resistance of freewheeling improvisers, softened in executive seminars, has apparently been worn down. The path from education to practice can be followed, for example, in the General Electric Company, where since 1964 an intensive course in general management has been offered at its Crotonville institute to the many potential general managers developed in the course of the company's operations and other development programs. When strategic planning was introduced into General Electric, beginning in 1970, the "strategic business unit," a combination of operations united by fundamental and long-range interconnections, ultimately became important in GE's management structure and processes. A series of strategic planning workshops for strategic planners was devised to prepare staff for the SBUs and to extend in procedural and substantive detail the earlier course in the formulation and evolution of corporate strategy. A thorough preparation for what is now often called *strategic management* has resulted in acceptance of the importance of making current decisions in the context of long-range plans.

The courses were designed and taught by professional educators. The organization structure and planning processes emerged from the work of a major consulting firm. The convergence of management education and consulting practice became acceptable because of the appearance of a concept of strategy which was recognized by experienced general managers as effective and powerful in practice.

Meanwhile similar developments elsewhere made *strategy* a favorite word, however unclear its meaning. The triumph of the concept has still a hollow sound, for the machinery of long-range planning has sometimes obscured critical choices, smothered innovation in financial analysis and hesitation, and produced line resistance to staff technocrats. When oversimplified in careless hands, portfolio analysis, for example, in which the various businesses of a multiproduct company are analyzed separately for their future prospects, leads more directly to classification and ranking of businesses than to determining their place, if any, in a unified company strategy. Growth and market-share goals and arbitrarily chosen financial objectives are sometimes mistaken for a considered statement of corporate purpose. Thoughtless use of the term has resulted in purposeless motion and distracting noise.

As its meaning has dispersed throughout recent usage, the word *strategy* still retains a close connection to a conscious purpose and implies a time dimension reaching into the future. At its simplest, a strategy can be a very specific plan of action directed at a specified result within a specified period of time. A sales force may develop a plan, for example, to take away an account from a competitor, in which the goal is to get its business by July 1980. What it plans to do is in this limited context a strategy; if a company is strategically managed it will be related at once to more comprehensive forms of marketing strategy like pricing. At any rate *functional strategy* (for example, in marketing, manufacturing, research and development, and finance) can be identified in any consciously managed company— it is the combination of purpose and policies that guides the conduct of the function. A marketing strategy in the company we just cited may be in part to lease its machinery in preference to selling it outright, but what its financial strategy is becomes of crucial importance in that case. The goal element of functional strategy is recognizable as natural to the function, like market share for marketing, efficiency for manufacturing, and return on investment for finance. But once again the interrelation of functional strategies determines their validity.

The term *business strategy* usually refers to the product-market choices made by division or product-line management in a diversified company. It comprises the combination of relevant functional strategies. The choice is presumably made after examining the behavior of competitors, the risks and opportunities in the market, the resources that can be coaxed out of the company, and the proven strength of the division. It is usually expressed in economic and competitive terms primarily and presupposes no discontinuity in the prospects or characteristics of the product concerned. Its time span is relatively short.

The concept of *corporate strategy*, which is defined below in Chapter 2, is comprehensive enough to include the business strategies guiding the divisions or product lines of a diversified company. Like business strategy, it includes both formulation and implementation, which interact upon each other. Like business strategy, it defines products and markets— and determines the company's course into the almost indefinite future. Sooner or later corporate strategy incorporates nonfinancial goals in organization, human, and ethical terms. A company will have only one corporate strategy but may incorporate into its concept of itself several business strategies.

This progression in the kinds of strategy recalls the accordion word *policy*, which can determine payment for overtime at one extreme or position a firm in its markets at the other. As we ascend from a specific strategy to corporate strategy, we pass from specific economic objectives to broader organization goals. More weight is given to such characteristics as unity, coherence, consistency, purpose, and concern for the future. The time horizon grows more distant and market-share percentages give way to a more comprehensive vision of the company's future development as an institution.

Although many variations in the use of a strategic vocabulary can be detected in any conversation in business or academic life, *strategic management* is becoming recognized as the administration of operations dominated by purpose and by consideration of future opportunity, with explicit attention given to the need to clarify or change strategy as results suggest and to enter the future on a predetermined course. Its most abstract form would be the supervision of the process within complex organizations through which strategy is formulated and monitored. *Strategic planning*, if used with *strategic management*, usually refers to the staff apparatus of long-range planning. Support activities like market research, evaluation of strategic alternatives, market performance and portfolio analysis, competitive intelligence, and environmental surveillance can fall within this activity. It can also be used to refer to all preparation for the future and as a synonym for the formulation (but not the achievement) of corporate strategy.

As this book will make clear, none of the modern paraphernalia of strategic planning need deter anyone from considering a simple practitioner's theory that begins in the determination of corporate purpose in economic, human, and social terms. The idea of corporate strategy brings all the special functions of business to bear on the highest function of the chief executive. It is capable of including the most extensive combination of interrelated variables involved in the most important of all business decisions.

This idea cannot be brought to final fruition in this book or any other. It is only in an industry, company, and specific situation that its power can be realized. As you experiment with its application to your own responsibilities you will encounter its advantages.

Clarification of the character and purposes of a company and establishing their linkage to all its operations have many uses. An articulate corporate strategy permits every company to distinguish itself from its competitors and establish a competitive advantage. It can keep the technical knowledge of the specialist focused on the primary purpose of the corporation rather than on the parochial concerns of technical functions. It requires conscious attention to the future equal in emphasis to the superficially more urgent demands of the present. It calls for the deliberate balancing of short-term and long-term considerations, which are usually in conflict. It exercises the mind and teases it out of complacence with success. It makes at least partially explicit the intuitive inclinations, judgments, and values that underlie business decisions and allows the inconsistency among them and their untested validity to be examined.

Needless to say, this book is more a record of the work of others than a creation of my own, just as were the notes in *Business Policy: Text and Cases.* I am longest in debt to C. Roland Christensen, with whom I work closely. Doing research and teaching together, we began long ago to see a way to generalize the situation-bound reality we were observing. Scores of others, colleagues at Harvard and elsewhere, in this country and overseas, have contributed to case and conceptual development. I will not attempt to name them here, for as the concept of strategy has spread through the teaching, research, and consulting of so many, it has lent power to their work without conspicuously retaining its theoretical identity or exacting loyalty to a jargon. The uses to which this idea is put have always seemed more important than its further theoretical development.

I acknowledge with gratitude the support offered to policy studies at the Harvard Business School by Dean John H. McArthur and all his predecessors.

March 1980   ***Kenneth R. Andrews***

 Contents

Chapter One

Chief executive officer,
president, or
general manager:
Roles and responsibilities

WHAT GENERAL MANAGEMENT IS

Management may be defined as the direction of informed, efficient, planned, and purposeful conduct of complex organized activity. General management is in its simplest form the management of a total enterprise or of an autonomous subunit. Its diverse forms in all kinds of businesses always include the integration of the work of functional managers or specialists.

The senior general manager in any organization is its chief executive officer; he or she may be called chairman of the board, president, or managing director. The title *general manager* may designate a less senior divisional or departmental post, but as a term may be used to designate all members of the hierarchy of general management—members of the office of the president, executive and senior vice presidents who have interfunctional responsibilities, and presidents or managers of divisions, multifunctional profit centers, and similar partially autonomous organization units. The point of view of general management, though not its full practice, is also essential to others—to outside directors, financial analysts, consultants, for example, who cannot accurately evaluate general management without knowing what it is. A total organization perspective is also important to senior functional officers whose concern is more for the contribution their subspecialists make to the operating organization than for the technical complexity of their work.

In this chapter we will examine the complexity of the general manager's job and the roles, functions, and skills that it requires. We are in quest of a point of view and organizing perspective that reduces to practicable order the otherwise impossible agenda of the chief executive of any organization—large or small.

COMPLEXITY OF GENERAL MANAGEMENT TASKS

General managers face such an array of functions and must exercise so varied a set of skills as to require a formidable versatility. If you were to see a successful entrepreneur invent and perfect a proprietary product, set up a company, devise a merchandising and distribution program of a very special kind suited to protect the product against substitutes, decide to maintain year-round production in a cyclical industry to meet the needs of a highly skilled work force, establish a research and development unit to make product diversification possible, set up methods of financing high inventory and rapid growth, recruit and put in place functional managers, and later choose a successor and withdraw from supervision of the company, you would necessarily conclude that such a general manager must be successful in a variety of roles. Consider the less varied case of a professionally trained MBA who moves up a functional hierarchy to become general manager of a division of the same organization 20 years after its founding. This person finds that the roles he or she plays and the responsibilities to be exercised within the roles differ according to the problem identified or the decision pending, the needs of the organization, or the needs and style of the president of the company. In either case the simple-minded adherence to one role—a personality-determined one, for example—will leave general managers miscast much of the time as the human drama they preside over unfolds.

We are in great need of a simple way to comprehend the total responsibility of chief executives. To multiply the list of tasks they must perform and the personal qualities they would do well to have would put general management capability beyond that of reasonably well-endowed human beings. Corporate presidents are accountable for everything that goes on in their organizations. They must preside over a total enterprise made up often of technical specialties in which they cannot possibly have personal expertness. They must know their company's markets and the ways in which they are changing. They must lead private lives as citizens in their communities and as family members, as individuals with their own needs and aspirations. Except for rare earlier experience, perhaps as general managers of profit centers in their own organizations, they have found no opportunity to practice being president before undertaking the office. New presidents are obliged to put behind them the specialized apparatus their education and functional experience have provided them. Engineers, for example, who continue to run their companies strictly as engineers will soon encounter financial and marketing problems, among others, that may force their removal.

Many attempts to characterize executive roles and functions come to very little, especially when they attempt to categorize in detail an almost infinite variety. The simplification that may best serve our approach to general management is to view its activities as assignable to three roles—*organization leader, personal leader, and architect of organization purpose.* As organization leader or manager of persons grouped in a hierarchy of suborganizations, the general manager can be called taskmaster, mediator, motivator, or organization designer, but theoretical distinctions among such illustrative categories become fruitless. The personal influence of leaders becomes evident as they play such roles as communicator, exemplar, or focus for respect or affection. The chief executive's role as architect of organization purpose is the principal subject of this book. This simple three-part separation of roles will enable us to identify the critical responsibilities and skills appropriate to each category. It is the reader's experience, recalled while reading, that will give these categories meaning and prepare the way for a new or more disciplined concept of management.

THE GENERAL MANAGER AS ORGANIZATION LEADER

Chief executives, presidents, chief operating officers, and general managers are first and probably least pleasantly persons who are responsible for results attained in the present as designated by plans made previously. Nothing that we will say shortly about their concern for the people in their organizations or later about their responsibility to society can gainsay this immediate truth. Achieving acceptable results against expectations of increased earnings per share and return on the stockholder's investment requires the general manager to be continually informed and ready to intervene when results fall below what had been expected. Changing circumstances and competition produce emergencies upsetting well-laid plans. Resourcefulness in responding to crisis is a skill which most successful executives develop early.

But the organizational consequences of the critical taskmaster role require executives to go beyond insistence upon achievement of planned results. They must see as their second principal function the creative maintenance and development of the organized capability that makes achievement possible. This activity leads to a third principle—the integration of the specialist functions which enable their organizations to perform the technical tasks in marketing, research and development, manufacturing, finance, control, and personnel, which proliferate as technology develops and tend to lead the company in all directions. If this coordination is successful in harmonizing special staff activities, general managers will probably have performed the task of getting organizations to accept and order priorities in accordance with the companies' objectives. Securing commitment to purpose is a central function of the president as organization leader.

The skills required by these functions reveal presidents not solely as taskmasters, but as mediators and motivators as well. They need ability in the education and motivation of people and the evaluation of their performance, two functions which tend to work against one another. The former requires understanding of individual needs, which persist no matter what the economic purpose of the organization. The latter requires objective assessment of the technical requirements of the task assigned. The capability required here is also that required in the integration of functions and the mediation of the conflict bound to arise out of technical specialism. The integrating capacity of the chief executive extends to meshing the economic, technical, human, and moral dimensions of corporate activity and to relating the company to its immediate and more distant communities. It will show itself in the formal organization designs which are put into effect as the blueprint of the required structured cooperation.

The perspective demanded of successful organization leaders embraces both the primacy of organization goals and the validity of individual goals. Besides this dual appreciation, they exhibit an impartiality toward the specialized functions and have criteria enabling them to allocate organization resources against documented needs. The point of view of the leader of an organization almost by definition requires an overview of its relations not only to its internal constituencies but to the relevant institutions and forces of its external environment. We will come soon to a conceptual solution of the problems encountered in the role of organizational leader.

THE PRESIDENT AS PERSONAL LEADER

The functions, skills, and relevant point of view of chief executives hold true no matter who they are or who makes up their organizations. The functions that accompany presidential performance of their role as communicator of purpose and policy, as exemplar, as the focal point for the respect or affection of subordinates vary much more according to personal energy, style, character, and integrity. Chief executives contribute as persons to the quality of life and performance in their organizations. This is true whether they are dynamic or colorless. By example they educate junior executives to seek to emulate them or simply to learn from their behavior what they really expect. They have the opportunity to infuse organized effort with flair or distinction if they have the skill to dramatize the relationship between their own activities and the goals of corporate effort.

All persons in leadership positions have or attain power which, in sophisticated organizations, they invoke as humanely and reasonably as possible in order to avoid the stultifying effects of dictatorship, dominance, or even markedly superior capacity. Formally announced policy, backed by the authority of the chief executive, can be made effective to some degree by clarity of direction, intensity of supervision, and the exercise of sanctions in enforcement. But in areas of judgment where policy cannot be specified without becoming absurdly overdetailed, chief executives establish by their own demeanor even more than in policy statements the moral and ethical level of performance expected. At the national level of executive behavior, one could see in the deportment of Presidents Kennedy, Johnson, Nixon, and Carter their real regard for the highest levels of ethical conduct. Failure of personal leadership in the White House leads to demoralization that is different only in scale and influence from what it is in the corporation. At the same time, however, no amount of personal integrity is sufficient without competence in organization leadership.

Formal correctness of structure and policy is not enough to inspire an organization. Enthusiasm for meeting ethical problems head on and avoiding shoddy solutions comes not so much from a system of rewards and punishments as from the sentiments of loyalty or courage stimulated by the personal deportment of the chief executive. By the persons they are, as much as by what they say and do, presidents influence their organizations and affect the development of individuals and the level of organized performance. At this juncture in the history of American business enterprise, conscious attention to the essential integrity of the chief executive becomes an important requirement if confidence in the corporate institutions of a democratic society is to be restored.

The skills of the effective personal leader are those of persuasion and articulation made possible by having something worth saying and by understanding the sentiments and points of view being addressed. Leaders cultivate and embody relationships between themselves and their subordinates appropriate to the style of leadership they have chosen or fallen into. Some of the qualities lending distinction to this leadership cannot be deliberately contrived, even by an artful schemer. The maintenance of personal poise in adversity or emergency and the capacity for development as an emotionally mature person are essential innate and developed capabilities. It is probably true that some personal preeminence in technical or social functions is either helpful or essential in demonstrating leadership related to the president's personal contribution. Credibility and cooperation depend upon demonstrated capacity of a kind more tangible and attractive, than, for example, the noiseless coordination of staff activity.

The relevant aspects of the presidential point of view brought to mind by activities in the role of personal leader are probably acknowledgment of one's personal needs and integrity as a person, and acceptance of the importance to others of their own points of view, behavior, and feelings. Self-awareness will acquaint leaders with their own personal strengths and weaknesses and keep them mindful of the inevitable unevenness of their own preparation for functions of general management. These qualities may be more important in the selection of a general manager than is the study of general management.

Michael Maccoby, author of The Gamesman, has conducted a provocative inquiry into executive character types.[1] He designates these as the Craftsman, the Jungle Fighter, the Company Man, and the Gamesman. The craftsman is dedicated to quality but unable to lead changing organizations. The jungle fighter is the anti-hero, who after rising rapidly is destroyed by those he has used. The company man is committed to corporate integrity and success but is said to lack the daring required to lead innovative organizations. The gamesman is the dominant type—able and enthusiastic, a team leader whose main goal is the exhilaration of victory. His main defect is said to be that his work has developed his intellectual but not his emotional gifts. Maccoby concedes that every person is a combination of types, but the flamboyant labels he uses to distinguish overlapping or coexisting traits produce an effect of caricature. Another effect of applying labels to roles is to suggest distances between them.

Despite these shortcomings, Maccoby's thesis that such qualities as generosity, idealism, and courage should accompany the gifts of the person devoted to a company and its objectives finds support in the work of psychoanalysts. If Maccoby is right in saying that the gamesman (by which he seems to mean quarterback or captain) is the representative type in leading American corporations today, then we have come a long way from the Carnegies, Rockefellers, and Astors of the 19th century. We still have a long way to go. The route passes directly through the pages that follow.

The prototype of the chief executive that we are developing is, in short, the able victory-seeking organizational leader who is making sure in what is done and the

---

[1]Michael Maccoby, The Gamesman (New York: Simon and Schuster, Inc., 1976). For a brief summary see "The Corporate Climber Has to Find His Heart," Fortune, December 1975, pp. 98–108.

changes pioneered in purpose and practice that the game is worth playing, the victory worth seeking, and life and career worth living. If the stature of corporation presidents as professional persons is not manifest in their concern for their organizations, they will not perform effectively over time in the role of either organization or personal leader. If we concede that the gamesman should be concerned with what the game is for, we are ready to consider the role of the chief executive in the choice of corporate objectives. That choice determines what the contest is about.

CHIEF EXECUTIVE AS ARCHITECT OF PURPOSE

To go beyond the organizational and personal roles of leadership, we enter the sphere of organization purpose, where we may find the atmosphere somewhat rare and the going less easy. The contribution senior executives make to their companies goes far beyond the apparently superficial activities that clutter their days.

Their attention to organization needs must extend beyond answering letters of complaint from spouses of aggrieved employees to appraisal (for example) of the impact of their companies' information, incentive, and control systems upon individual behavior. Their personal contribution to their company goes far beyond easily understood attention to key customers and speeches to the Economic Club to the more subtle influence their own probity and character have on subordinates. We must turn now to activities even further out—away from immediate everyday decisions and emergencies. Some part of what a president does is oriented toward maintaining the development of a company over time and preparing for a future more distant than the time horizon appropriate to the roles and functions identified thus far.

The most difficult role—and the one we will concentrate on henceforth—of the chief executive of any organization is the one in which he serves as custodian of corporate objectives. The entrepreneurs who create a company know at the outset what they are up to. Their objectives are intensely personal, if not exclusively economic, and their passions may be patent protection and finance. If they succeed in passing successfully through the phase of personal entrepreneurship, where they or their bankers or families are likely to be the only members of the organization concerned with purpose, they find themselves in the role of planner, managing the process by which ideas for the future course of the company are conceived, evaluated, fought over, and accepted or rejected.

The presidential functions involved include establishing or presiding over the goal-setting and resource-allocation processes of the company, making or ratifying choices among strategic alternatives, and clarifying and defending the goals of the company against external attack or internal erosion. The installation of purpose in place of improvisation and the substitution of planned progress in place of drifting are probably the most demanding functions of the president. Successful organization leadership requires great human skill, sensitivity, and administrative ability. Personal leadership is built upon personality and character. The capacity for determining and monitoring the adequacy of the organization's continuing purposes implies as well analytic intelligence of a high order. The chief executive we are talking about is not a two-dimensional poster or television portrait. Neither are the subordinates who help him most.

The crucial skill of the general manager concerned

with corporate purpose includes the creative generation or recognition of strategic alternatives made valid by developments in the marketplace and the capability and resources of the company. Along with this, in a combination not easily come by, runs the critical capacity to analyze the strengths and weaknesses of documented proposals. The ability to perceive with some objectivity corporate strengths and weaknesses is essential to sensible choice of goals, for the most attractive goal is not attainable without the strength to open the way to it through inertia and intense opposition, with all else that lies between.

Probably the skill most nearly unique to general management, as opposed to the management of functional or technical specialties, is the intellectual capacity to conceptualize corporate purpose and the dramatic skill to invest it with some degree of magnetism. No sooner is a distinctive set of corporate objectives vividly delineated than the temptation to go beyond it sets in. Under some circumstances it is the chief executive's function to defend properly focused purpose against superficially attractive diversification or corporate growth that glitters like fool's gold. Because defense of proper strategy can be interpreted as mindless conservatism, wholly appropriate defense of a still valid strategy requires courage, supported by detailed documentation.

Continuous monitoring, in any event, of the quality and continued suitability of corporate purpose is over time the most sophisticated and essential of all the functions of general management alluded to here. Because of its difficulty and vulnerability to current emergency, you will be able to identify lost opportunities for this activity from your own experience. Everyone can. Because of its low visibility, you may not have noticed when this activity was being followed. The perspective which sustains this function is the kind of creative discontent which prevents complacency even in good times and seeks continuous advancement of corporate and individual capacity and performance. It requires also constant attention to the future, as if the present did not offer problems and opportunities enough.

ENORMITY OF THE TASK

Even so sketchy a record of what a president is called upon to do is likely to seem an academic idealization, given the disparity between the complexity of role and function and the modest qualifications of those impressed into the office. Like the Molière character who discovered that for 40 years he had been speaking prose without knowing it, many managers have been programmed by instinct and experience to the kind of performance which we have attempted to decipher here. For those less experienced, the catalog may seem impossibly long.

Essentially, however, we have looked at only three major roles and four sets of responsibilities. The roles deal with the requirements for organizational and personal leadership and for conscious attention to the formulation and promulgation of purpose. The four groups of functions encompass (1) securing the attainment of planned results in the present, (2) developing an organization capable of producing both technical achievement and human satisfactions, (3) making a distinctive personal contribution, and (4) planning and executing policy decisions affecting future results.

Even thus simplified, how to apply this identification

of presidential role and function to the incomparably detailed confusion of a national or international company situation cannot possibly be made clear in the process of generalization. But we have come to the central importance of purpose. The theory presented here begins with the assumption that in every organization (corporate or otherwise), every subunit of organization, every group and individual should be guided by an evolving set of goals which permit movement in a chosen direction and prevent drifting.

NEED FOR A CONCEPT

The complexity of the general manager's job and the desirability of raising intuitive competence to the level of verifiable, conscious, and systematic analysis suggest the need, as indicated earlier, for a unitary concept as useful to the generalist as the canons of technical functions are to the specialist. We will propose shortly a simple practitioner's theory which we hope will reduce the four-faceted responsibility of the company's senior executives to more reasonable proportions, make it susceptible to objective research and systematic evaluation, and bring to more well-qualified people the skills it requires. The central concept we call "corporate strategy." It will be required to embrace the entire corporation, to take shape in the terms and conditions in which its business is conducted. It will be constructed from the points of view described so far. Central to this Olympian vantage point is impartiality with respect to the value of individual specialties, including the one through which the executive rose to generalist responsibilities. It will insist upon the values of the special functions in proportion to their contribution to corporate purpose and ruthlessly dispense with those not crucially related to the objectives sought. It necessarily will define the chief executive's role in such a way as to allow delegation of much of the general management responsibility described here without loss of clarity. Our hope will be to make challenging but practicable the connection between the highest priority for goal setting and a durable but flexible definition of a company's goals and major company-determining policies. How to define, decide, put into effect, and defend a conscious strategy appropriate to emerging market opportunity and company capability will then take precedence over and lend order to the fourfold functions of general management here presented.

Despite a shift in emphasis toward the anatomy of a concept and the development of an analytical approach to the achievement of valid corporate strategy, we will not forget the chief executive's special role in contributing quality to purpose through standards exercised in the choice of what to do and the way in which it is to be done and through the projection of *quality* as a person. It will remain true, after we have taken apart the process by which strategy is conceived, that executing it at a high professional level will depend upon the depth and durability of the chief executive's personal values, standards of quality, and clarity of character. We will return in a final comment on the management of the strategic process to the truth that the president's function above all is to be the exemplar of a permanent human aspiration—the determination to devote one's powers to jobs worth doing. Conscious attention to corporate strategy will be wasted if it does not elevate the quality of corporate purpose and achievement.

Chapter two

The concept of
corporate strategy

We come at last to the simple central concept called corporate strategy. Henceforth we will be concerned with deciding what it is as idea and management process and how in a company to formulate, evaluate, and implement it. In this chapter we will examine the comprehensive definition I propose as the most useful, the terms in which strategy should be stated to make sense, the forms different kinds of strategy take in different kinds of companies, and the tests of validity that may be applied to it.

WHAT STRATEGY IS

Corporate strategy is the pattern of decisions in a company that determines and reveals its objectives, purposes, or goals, produces the principal policies and plans for achieving those goals, and defines the range of business the company is to pursue, the kind of economic and human organization it is or intends to be, and the nature of the economic and noneconomic contribution it intends to make to its shareholders, employees, customers, and communities. In an organization of any size or diversity, "corporate strategy" usually applies to the whole enterprise, while "business strategy," less comprehensive, defines the choice of product or service and market of individual businesses within the firm. Business strategy, that is, is the determination of how a company will compete in a given business and position itself among its competitors. Corporate strategy defines the businesses in-which a company will compete, preferably in a way that focuses resources to convert distinctive competence into competitive advantage. Both are outcomes of a continuous process of strategic management that we will later analyze in detail.

The strategic decision contributing to this pattern is one that is effective over long periods of time, affects the company in many different ways, and focuses and commits a significant portion of its resources to the expected outcomes. The pattern resulting from a series of such decisions will probably define the central character and image of a company, the individuality it has for its members and various publics, and the position it will occupy in its industry and markets. It will permit the specification of particular objectives to be attained through a timed sequence of investment and implementation decisions and will govern directly the deployment or redeployment of resources to make these decisions effective.

Some aspects of such a pattern of decision may be in an established corporation unchanging over long periods of time, like a commitment to quality, or high technology, or certain raw materials, or good labor relations. Other aspects of a strategy must change as or before the world changes, such as product line, manufacturing process, or merchandising and styling practices. The basic determinants of company character, if purposefully institutionalized, are likely to persist through and shape the nature of substantial changes in product-market choices and allocation of resources.

It would be possible to extend the definition of strategy for a given company to separate a central character and the core of its special accomplishment from the manifestations of such characteristics in changing product lines, markets, and policies designed to make activities profitable from year to year. *The New York Times*, for example, after many years of being shaped by the values of its owners and staff, is now so self-conscious and respected an institution that its nature is likely to remain unchanged, even if the services it offers are altered drastically in the direction of other outlets for its news-processing capacity.

It is important, however, not to take the idea apart in another way, i.e. to separate goals from the policies designed to achieve those goals. The essence of the definition of strategy I have just recorded is *pattern*. The interdependence of purposes, policies, and organized action is crucial to the particularity of an individual strategy and its opportunity to identify competitive advantage. It is the unity, coherence, and internal consistency of a company's strategic decisions that position the company in its environment and give the firm its identity, its power to mobilize its strengths, and its likelihood of success in the marketplace. It is the interrelationship of a set of goals and policies that crystallizes from the formless reality of a company's environment a set of problems an organization can seize upon and solve.

What you are doing, in short, is never meaningful unless you can say or imply what you are doing it for: the quality of administrative action and the motivation lending it power cannot be appraised without knowing its relationship to purpose. Breaking up the system of corporate goals and the character-determining major policies for attainment leads to narrow and mechanical conceptions of strategic management and endless logic-chopping.

We should get on to understanding the need for strategic decision and for determining the most satisfactory pattern of goals in concrete instances. Refinement of

definition can wait, for you will wish to develop definition in practice in directions useful to you.

SUMMARY STATEMENTS OF STRATEGY

Before we proceed to clarification of this concept by
application, we should specify the terms in which
strategy is usually expressed. A summary statement of
strategy will characterize the product line and services
offered or planned by the company, the markets and market segments for which products and services are now or
will be designed, and the channels through which these
markets will be reached. The means by which the operation is to be financed will be specified, as will the profit
objectives and the emphasis to be placed on the safety of
capital versus level of return. Major policy in central
functions such as marketing, manufacturing, procurement, research and development, labor relations, and
personnel, will be stated where they distinguish the
company from others, and usually the intended size,
form, and climate of the organization will be included.

Each company, if it were to construct a summary
strategy from what it understands itself to be aiming at,
would have a different statement with different categories
of decision emphasized to indicate what it wanted to be
or do.

To indicate the nature of such a statement, a student of
a famous old policy case on the Heublein company deduced this statement from the account of the company
when it was much smaller and less diversified than it is
now and was about to make the mistake of acquiring
Hamm's Brewery:

Heublein aims to market in the U.S. and via franchise overseas a wide variety of high margin, high quality consumer products concentrated in the liquor and food business, especially bottled cocktails, vodka, and other special-use and distinctive beverages and specialty convenience foods, addressed to a relatively prosperous, young-adult market and returning over 15 percent of equity after taxes. With emphasis on the techniques of consumer goods marketing [brand promotion, wide distribution, product representation in more than one price segment, and very substantial off-beat advertising directed closely to its growing audience] Heublein intends to make Smirnoff the number one liquor brand worldwide via internal growth [and franchise] or acquisitions or both. Its manufacturing policy rather than full integration is in liquor to redistill only to bring purchased spirits up to high quality standards. It aims to finance its internal growth through the use of debt and its considerable cash flow and to use its favorable price earnings ratio for acquisitions. Both its liquor and food distribution are intended to secure distributor support through advertising and concern for the distributor's profit.

Although it might be argued that the statement was not clearly in the chief executive's mind when he contemplated purchasing Hamm's Brewery and therefore did not help him refrain from that decision, it was in his experience and in the pattern of the company's past strategic decisions—at least as reported in the case. In many ways incomplete (no mention is made of organization or social responsibility sub-strategies) this statement does make possible a large question about the beer business as a compatible element in the company's marketing mix.

REASONS FOR NOT ARTICULATING STRATEGY

For a number of reasons companies seldom formulate and publish as complete a statement even as the one we have just illustrated. Conscious planning of the long-term development of companies has been until recently less common than individual executive responses to environmental pressure, competitive threat, or entrepreneurial opportunity. In the latter mode of development, the unity or coherence of corporate effort is unplanned, natural, intuitive, or even nonexistent. Incrementalism in practice sometimes gives the appearance of consciously formulated strategy, but may be the natural result of compromise among coalitions backing contrary policy proposals or skillful improvisatory adaptation to external forces. Practicing managers who prefer muddling through to the strategic process would never commit themselves to an articulate strategy.

Other reasons for the scarcity of concrete statements of strategy include the desirability of keeping strategic plans confidential for security reasons and ambiguous to avoid internal conflict or even final decision. Skillful incrementalists may have plans in their heads which they do not reveal, to avoid resistance and other trouble in their own organization. A company with a large division in an obsolescent business which it intends to drain of cash until operations are discontinued could not expect high morale and cooperation to follow publication of this intent. In a dynamic company, moreover, where strategy is continually evolving, the official statement of strategy, unless it was couched in very general terms, would be as hard to keep up to date as an organization chart. Finally, a firm that has internalized its strategy does not feel the need to keep saying what it is, valuable as that information might be to new members.

DEDUCING STRATEGY FROM BEHAVIOR

In your own company you can do what most managements have not done. In the absence of explicit statements and on the basis of your experience, you may deduce from decisions observed what the pattern is and what the company's goals and policies are, on the assumption that some perhaps unspoken consensus lies behind them. Careful examination of the behavior of competitors will reveal what their strategy must be. At the same time none of us should mistake apparent strategy visible in a pattern of past incremental decisions for conscious planning for the future. What will pass as the current strategy of a company may almost always be deduced from its behavior, but a strategy for a future of changed circumstance may not always be distinguishable from performance in the present. Strategists who do not look beyond present behavior to the future are vulnerable to surprise.

FORMULATION OF STRATEGY

Corporate strategy is an organization process, in many ways inseparable from the structure, behavior, and culture of the company in which it takes place. Nevertheless, we may abstract from the process two important aspects, interrelated in real life but separable for the purposes of analysis. The first of these we may call *formulation*, the second *implementation*. Deciding what strategy should be may be approached as a rational undertaking, even if in life emotional attachments (as to metal skis or investigative reporting) may complicate choice among future alternatives (for ski manufacturers or alternative newspapers). The principal subactivities of strategy formulation as a logical activity include identifying opportunities and threats in the company's environment and attaching some estimate or risk to the discernible alternatives. Before a choice can be made, the company's strengths and weaknesses should be appraised together with the resources on hand and available. Its actual or potential capacity to take advantage of perceived market needs or to cope with attendant risks should be estimated as objectively as possible. The strategic alternative which results from matching opportunity and corporate capability at an acceptable level of risk is what we may call an *economic strategy*.

The process described thus far assumes that strategists are analytically objective in estimating the relative capacity of their company and the opportunity they see or anticipate in developing markets. The extent to which they wish to undertake low or high risk presumably depends on their profit objectives. The higher they set the latter, the more willing they must be to assume a correspondingly high risk that the market opportunity they see will not develop or that the corporate competence required to excel competition will not be forthcoming.

So far we have described the intellectual processes of ascertaining what a company *might do* in terms of environmental opportunity, of deciding what it *can do* in terms of ability and power, and of bringing these two considerations together in optimal equilibrium. The determination of strategy also requires consideration of what alternatives are preferred by the chief executive and perhaps by his or her immediate associates as well, quite apart from economic considerations. Personal values, aspirations, and ideals do, and in our judgment quite properly should, influence the final choice of purposes. Thus what the executives of a company *want to do* must be brought into the strategic decision.

Finally strategic choice has an ethical aspect—a fact much more dramatically illustrated in some industries than in others. Just as alternatives may be ordered in terms of the degree of risk that they entail, so may they be examined against the standards of responsiveness to the expectations of society that the strategist elects. Some alternatives may seem to the executive considering them more attractive than others when the public good or service to society is considered. What a company *should do* thus appears as a fourth element of the strategic decision.

The ability to identify the four components of strategy—(1) market opportunity, (2) corporate competence and resources, (3) personal values and aspirations, and (4) acknowledged obligations to segments of society other than stockholders—is easier to exercise than the art of reconciling their implications in a final choice of purpose. Taken by itself each consideration might lead in a different direction.

If you put the various aspirations of individuals in your own organization against this statement you will see what I mean. Even in a single mind contradictory aspirations can survive a long time before the need to calculate trade-offs and integrate divergent inclinations becomes clear. Growth opportunity attracted many companies to the computer business after World War II. The decision to diversify out of typewriters and calculators was encouraged by growth opportunity and excitement which captivated the managements of RCA, General Electric, and

Xerox, among others. But the financial, technical, and marketing requirements of this business exceeded the capacity of most of the competitors of IBM. The magnet of opportunity and the incentive of desire obscured the calculations of what resources and competence were required to succeed. Most crucially, where coporate capability leads, executives do not always want to go. Of all the components of strategic choice, the combination of resources and competence is most crucial to success.

THE IMPLEMENTATION OF STRATEGY

Since faulty implementation can make a sound strategic decision ineffective and skilled implementation can make a debatable choice successful, it is as important to examine the processes of implementation as to weigh the advantages of available strategic alternatives. The implementation of strategy is comprised of a series of subactivities which are primarily administrative. If purpose is determined, then the resources of a company can be mobilized to accomplish it. An organizational structure appropriate for the efficient performance of the required tasks must be made effective by information systems and relationships permitting coordination of subdivided activities. The organizational processes of performance measurement, compensation, management development— all of them enmeshed in systems of incentives and controls—must be directed toward the kind of behavior required by organizational purpose. The role of personal leadership is important and sometimes decisive in the accomplishment of strategy. Although we know that organization structure and processes of compensation, incentives, control, and management development influence and constrain the formulation of strategy, we should look first at the logical proposition that structure should follow strategy in order to cope later with the organizational reality that strategy also follows structure. When we have examined both tendencies, we will understand and to some extent be prepared to deal with the interdependence of the formulation and implementation of corporate purpose. Figure 1 may be useful in understanding the analysis of strategy as a pattern of interrelated decisions.

KINDS OF STRATEGIES

The most important characteristics of a corporate pattern of decision that may properly be called strategic is its uniqueness. A creative reconciliation of alternatives for future development is made unique by the special characteristics of an organization, its central competence, history, financial and technical resources, and the aspirations and sense of responsibility of its leaders. The environment—market opportunity and risk—is more

FIGURE 1

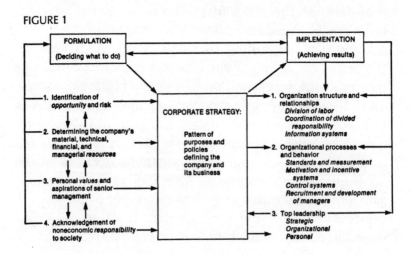

nearly the same for major companies operating in the same geographical regions than are the resources, values, and responsibility components of strategy. For the company unequipped to dominate the full range of opportunity, the quest for a profitable segment of, or niche in, a market is, if successful, also likely to distinguish one company from another. In fact in an industry where all companies seem to have the same strategy, we will find trouble for all but the leaders—as at various times American Motors, Chrysler, and Ford have had different degrees of difficulty following General Motors, which got where it is by *not* following the previous industry leader, Henry Ford.[1]

Nonetheless it is useful to have in mind the full range of possible strategies when the question is posed whether the present strategy is the best possible. When you begin to consider other possibilities, the generation of alternatives will take place within the following commonsense range of possibilities.

Low-growth strategies

1. *No change.*   The strategy properly identified and checked out against the tests of validity outlined below can be closely monitored, fine-tuned for minor defects, managed for maximum cash flows, with low investment in forced growth. Defensive contingencies will be designed for unexpected change, and efficient implementation will be the focus of top management attention. Since the recession of the mid-70s, and the onset of conservation and environmental protection, this strategy is more

---

[1]For a basic study in strategy formulation, see Alfred P. Sloan, *My Years at General Motors* (Garden City, N.Y.: Doubleday & Co., Inc., 1964).

attractive than it was in the heyday of "more is better."
The profit to be made from doing better what a company
already knows how to do rather than investing heavily in
growth is the attraction of this strategy, which can be protected by achievement of low costs. Its disadvantage is
the possibility of being overtaken or displaced by new
development and the restriction of opportunity for organization members.

2. *Retreat.*   The possibility of liquidation is not to be
sought out, but may for companies in deep trouble be a
better choice than continuing the struggle. Less drastic
alternatives than complete liquidation include discon-
tinuance or divestment of marginal operations, or merg-
ing with a ceding of management control.

3. *Focus on limited special opportunity.*   A more
constructive course of contraction is concentration on a
profitable specialty product or a limited but significant
market niche. Success in a narrow line almost always
tempts a company to broaden its line, but the McIlhenny
strategy (Tabasco sauce only) may not be totally obsolete.
If the proper focus is chosen, the limits may relax and
growth may come in any case. Once the risk of limited life
is accepted, the advantages of the no-change strategy can
be sought.

Forced-growth strategies

1. *Acquisition of competitors.*   In the early states of
its development, a company with a successful strategy
and proven record of successful execution can acquire
small competitors in the same business to expand its
market. Eventually antitrust regulation will put an end to
this practice, unless the prospective acquisition is very

small or on the edge of bankruptcy. Such acquisitions are usually followed by an adaptation of strategy either by the parent or acquired company to keep the total company a single business or one dominated by its original product-market specialization.

2. *Vertical integration.*   A conservative growth strategy, keeping a company close to its core competence and experience in its industry, consists of moving backward via acquisition or internal development to sources of supply and forward toward the ultimate customer. When a newspaper buys a pulp and paper mill and forest lands or news agencies for distribution, it is extending its strategy but not changing materially the nature of its business. Increasing the stages of integration provides a greater number of options to be developed or closed out as, for example, the making of fine paper and the distribution of magazines.

3. *Geographical expansion.*   Enlargement of territory can be accomplished by building new plants and enlarging marketing organizations or by acquisition of competitors. For a sizeable company the opportunity to enlarge international operations by export, establishments of plants and marketing activities overseas, with or without foreign partners, may protect against contraction forced by domestic competition.

4. *Diversification.*   The avenue to growth which presents the most difficult strategic choices is diversification. Diversification can range from minor additions to a company's basic product line to the acquisition of completely unrelated businesses. It can be sought through internal research and development, the purchase of new product ideas or technology, and the acquisition of companies.

KINDS OF COMPANIES

The process of strategic decision differs in complexity depending upon the diversity of the company in question. Just as having in mind the range of strategy from liquidation to multinational diversification will stimulate the generation of strategic alternatives, so a simple way of differentiating kinds of companies will help us see why different kinds of companies have different kinds of problems in making their activities coherent and effective and in setting a course for the future.

Bruce Scott of the Harvard Business School has developed a model of stages of corporate development in which each stage is characterized by the way a firm is managed and the scope of strategic choice available to it. *Stage I* is a single-product (or line of products) company with little or no formal structure run by the owner, who personally performs most of the managerial functions using subjective and unsystematic measures of performance and reward and control systems. The strategy of this firm is what the owner-manager wants it to be.

Stage II is the single-product firm grown so large that functional specialization has become imperative. A degree of integration has developed between raw materials, production processes, distribution, and sales. The search for product or process improvement is institutionalized in research and development, and performance management and control and compensation systems become systematic with the formulation of policy to guide delegation of operating decisions. The strategic choice is still under top control and centers upon the degree of integration, size of market share, and breadth of product line.

Stage III is a company with multiple product lines and channels of distribution, with an organization based on

product-market relationships rather than function. Its
businesses are not to a significant degree integrated; they
have their own markets. Its research and development is
oriented to new products rather than improvements, and
its measurement and control systems are increasingly
systematic and oriented to results. Strategic alternatives
are phrased in terms of entry into and exit from industries, and allocation of resources by industry and rate of
growth.

If a company grows it may pass from Stage I to Stage III,
although it can be very large in Stage II. Its strategic decisions will grow in complexity. The stages of development
model has proved productive in relating different kinds
of strategies to kinds of companies and has led other researchers into productive classification. Leonard Wrigley
and Richard P. Rumelt have carried Scott's work forward
to develop suggestive ways of categorizing companies
and comparing their strategies.[2]

First, of course, is the *single business* firm (Stages I and
II firms) with 95 percent or more of its revenues arising
from a single business—an oil, flour-milling, or metal
container company, for example.

Second is the *dominant business* firm, diversified to
some extent but still obtaining most of its revenues from a
single business. The diversification may arise from end
products of integration, with products stemming from
strengths of the firm, or from minor unrelated activities.
A large oil company in the petrochemical and fertilizer
business would fall in this category.

---

[2]Leonard Wrigley, "Division Autonomy and Diversification" (unpublished
doctoral dissertation, Harvard Business School, 1970) and Richard P. Rumelt,
Strategy Structure and Economic Performance (Division of Research, Harvard
Business School, 1974). Malcolm Salter has added a refinement to Stage III in
"Stages of Corporate Development," *Journal of Business Policy*, vol. 1, no. 1
(1970), pp. 40–51.

Third is the *related business* firm in which the diversification has been principally accomplished by relating new activities to old—General Electric and Westinghouse, for example.

Fourth is the *unrelated business* firm. These firms have diversified primarily without regard to relationships between new businesses and current activities. The conglomerate companies fall in this category.

It is interesting to note that Rumelt has found significant superior performance in the related business firms, suggesting that the strategy of diversifying from the original business to a significant degree but staying within the sphere of established competence has been the most successful strategic pattern among the *Fortune 500* under conditions prevailing in recent years. Unfortunately, familiar problems in establishing causation prevent final conclusions.

The range of strategy and the kinds of company which different growth strategies have produced suggest, in short, that the process of defining the business of a company will vary greatly depending on the degree of diversification under way in the company. The product-market choices are crystal clear in a single business oil company; they could not even be listed for General Electric. That top management actually decides product-market questions in such a company, except in such instances as entry into nuclear energy, is conceivable only as an oversimplification.

As diversification increases, the definition of the total business turns away from literal description of products and markets (which becomes the business of the separate product divisions) toward general statements of financial results expected and corporate principle in other areas. A conglomerate firm made up of many different businesses will have many different business strategies, related or not depending upon the desire for synergy in the strategic direction of the total enterprise. The overall common strategy of a highly diversified firm may be only the total of its divisional strategies. That it should be more than that is a matter for argument. To make it so puts heavy demands on the ability to conceptualize corporate purpose.

The task of identifying the coherence and unity of a conglomerate is, of course, much greater than doing so for even a multidivision related business. You should be prepared, then, to adapt the beginning definition offered here to the complexity of the business you are examining. Since the trend over time is product diversity in growing firms and evolution from Stage I to Stage III, it is well to have this complication in mind now.

For as Norman Berg makes clear in "Strategic Planning in Conglomerate Companies," strategic choice is not merely the function of the chief executive office.[3] It is of necessity a multilevel activity, with each unit concerned with its own environment and its own objectives. The process will reflect the noneconomic goals of people at the level at which proposals are made. In a conglomerate of unrelated businesses the corporate staff is small, the division relatively autonomous, and the locus of strategic planning is in the divisions. This makes supervision of the strategic planning process and allocation of resources, depending upon the evaluation of strategies submitted, the strategic role of the corporate senior managers.

---

[3]Norman Berg, "Strategic Planning in Conglomerate Companies," *Harvard Business Review*, May–June 1965, pp. 79–92. See also his "What's Different about Conglomerate Management?" *Harvard Business Review*, November–December 1969)

The differences in the application of a concept of strategy to a modest single business on the one hand and to a multinational conglomerate on the other—although important—mean that the ability to conceive of a business in strategic terms must be distributed throughout the organization in a complex company. The problems of choosing among strategic alternatives and making the choice effective over time, together with the problems of ensuring that such organization processes as performance measurement do not impede the choice, must be a familiar part of the management tasks of many people besides the general managers. All those involved in the strategic process, it follows, are vitally concerned with how a strategy can be evaluated so that it may be continued, amended, or abandoned as appropriate. Operating level managers who make a strategic proposal should be able to test its validity against corporate norms if for no other reason than their own survival. Those who must approve and allocate funds to such proposals should have a criterion to evaluate their worth going beyond a general confidence (or lack of it) in the ability of the proponents.

CRITERIA FOR EVALUATION

How is the actual or proposed strategy to be judged? How are we to know that one strategy is better than another? A number of important questions can regularly be asked. As is already evident, no infallible indicators are available. With practice they will lead to reliable intuitive discriminations.

1. *Is the strategy identifiable and has it been made clear either in words or in practice?*

The degree to which attention has been given to the

strategic alternatives available to a company is likely to be basic to the soundness of its strategic decision. To cover in empty phrases ("Our policy is planned profitable growth in any market we can serve well") an absence of analysis of opportunity or actual determination of corporate strength is worse than to remain silent, for it conveys the illusion of a commitment when none has been made. The unstated strategy cannot be tested or contested and is likely therefore to be weak. If it is implicit in the intuition of a strong leader, the organization is likely to be weak and the demands the strategy makes upon it are likely to remain unmet. A strategy must be explicit to be effective and specific enough to require some actions and exclude others.

2.   *Does the strategy exploit fully domestic and international environmental opportunity?*

An unqualified yes answer is likely to be rare even in the instance of such global giants as General Motors. But the present and future dimensions of markets can be analyzed without forgetting the limited resources of the company in order to outline the requirements of balanced growth and the need for environmental information. The relation between market opportunity and organizational development is a critical one in the design of future plans. Unless growth is incompatible with the resources of an organization or the aspirations of its management, it is likely that a strategy that does not purport to make full use of market opportunity will be weak also in other aspects. Vulnerability to competition is increased by lack of interest in market share.

3.   *Is the strategy consistent with corporate competence and resources, both present and projected?*

Although additional resources, both financial and managerial, are available to companies with genuine opportunity, the availability of each must be finally determined and programmed along a practicable time scale. This may be the most difficult question in this series. The key factor which is usually left out is the availability of management for effective implementation or the opportunity cost implicit in the assignment of management to any task. It is also very difficult to assess distinctive competence, and few companies have done it to the satisfaction of more than one person.

4. *Are the major provisions of the strategy and the program of major policies of which it is comprised internally consistent?*

A foolish consistency, Emerson said, is the hobgoblin of little minds, and consistency of any kind is certainly not the first qualification of successful corporation presidents. Nonetheless, one advantage of making as specific a statement of strategy as is practicable is the resultant availability of a careful check on fit, unity, coherence, compatibility, and synergy—the state in which the whole of anything can be viewed as greater than the sum of its parts. For example, a manufacturer of chocolate candy who depends for two thirds of his business upon wholesalers should not follow a policy of ignoring them or of dropping all support of their activities and all attention to their complaints. Similarly, two engineers who found a new firm expressly to do development work should not follow a policy of accepting orders that, though highly profitable, in effect turn their company into a large job shop, with the result that unanticipated financial and production problems take all the time that might have gone into development. An examination of any substantial firm will reveal at least some details in which policies pursued by different departments tend to go in different directions. Where inconsistency threatens concerted effort to achieve budgeted results within a planned time period, then consistency becomes a vital rather than merely an esthetic problem.

5. *Is the chosen level of risk feasible in economic and personal terms?*

Strategies vary in the degree of risk willingly undertaken by their designers. For example, a small food company in pursuit of its marketing strategy deliberately courted disaster in production slowdowns and in erratic behavior of cocoa futures. But the choice was made knowingly and the return was likely to be correspondingly great. The president was temperamentally able to live under this pressure and presumably had recourse if disaster struck. At the other extreme, another company had such modest growth aspirations that the junior members of its management were unhappy. They would have preferred a more aggressive and ambitious company. Although risk cannot always be known for sure, the level at which it is estimated is, within limits, optional. The riskiness of any future plan should be compatible with the economic resources of the organization and the temperament of the managers concerned.

6. *Is the strategy appropriate to the personal values and aspirations of the key managers?*

Until we consider the relationship of personal values to the choice of strategy, it is not useful to dwell long upon this criterion. But, to cite an extreme case, the deliberate falsification of warehouse receipts to conceal the absence of soybean oil from the tanks which are supposed to contain it would not be an element of competitive strategy to which most of us would like to be committed. A strong personal attraction of leisure, to cite a less extreme example, is inconsistent with a strategy requiring all-out effort from the senior members of a company. Or if, for example, a new president abhors conflict and competition, then it can be predicted that the hard-driven firm of an earlier day will have to change its strategy when he takes over. Conflict between personal preferences, aspirations, and goals of the key members of an organization and the plan for its future is a sign of danger and a harbinger of mediocre performance or failure.

7.   *Is the strategy appropriate to the desired level of contribution to society?*

Closely allied to the value is the ethical criterion. As the professional obligations of business are acknowledged by an increasing number of senior managers, it grows more and more appropriate to ask whether the current strategy of a firm is as socially responsible as it might be. Although it can be argued that filling any economic need contributes to the social good, it is clear that manufacturers of cigarettes might well consider diversification on grounds other than their fear of future legislation. That the strategy should not require violations of law or ethical practice to be effective has become abundantly clear with the revelation in the mid-70s of widespread bribery and questionable payments, particularly in overseas activities. Honesty and integrity may seem exclusively questions of implementation, but if the strategy is not distinctive, making it effective in competition may tempt managers to unethical practice. Thus a drug manufacturer who emphasizes the production of amphetamines at a level beyond total established medical need is inevitably compelling corruption. The meeting of sales quotas at the distribution level necessitates distribution of the drug as "speed" with or without the cooperation of prescribing physicians. To the extent that the chosen economic opportunity of the firm has social costs, such as air or water pollution, a statement of intention to deal with these is desirable and prudent. Ways to ask and answer this question will be considered in the section on the company and its responsibilities to society.

8.   *Does the strategy constitute a clear stimulus to organizational effort and commitment?*

For organizations which aspire not merely to survive but to lead and to generate productive performance in a climate that will encourage the development of competence and the satisfaction of individual needs, the strategy selected should be examined for its inherent attractiveness to the organization. Some undertakings are inherently more likely to gain the commitment of able men of goodwill than others. Given the variety of human preferences, it is risky to illustrate this difference briefly. But currently a company that is vigorously expanding its overseas operations finds that several of its socially conscious young people exhibit more zeal in connection with its work in developing countries than in Europe. Generally speaking, the bolder the choice of goals and the wider range of human needs they reflect, the more successfully they will appeal to the capable membership of a healthy and energetic organization.

9.   *Are there early indications of the responsiveness of markets and market segments to the strategy?*

Results, no matter how long postponed by necessary preparations, are, of course, the most telling indicators of soundness, so long as they are read correctly at the proper time. A strategy may pass with flying colors all the tests so far proposed, and may be in internal consistency and uniqueness an admirable work of art. But if within a time period made reasonable by the company's resources and the original plan the strategy does not work, then it must be weak in some way that has escaped attention. Bad luck, faulty implementation, and competitive counter-moves may be more to blame for unsatisfactory results than flaws in design, but the possibility of the latter should not be unduly discounted. Conceiving a strategy that will win the company a unique place in the business community, that will give it an enduring concept of itself, that will harmonize its diverse activities, and that will provide a fit between environmental opportunity and present or potential company strength is an extremely complicated task.

We cannot expect simple tests of soundness to tell the whole story. But an analytical examination of any company's strategy against the several criteria here suggested will nonetheless give anyone concerned with making, proving, or contributing to corporate planning a good deal to think about.

PROBLEMS IN EVALUATION

The evaluation of strategy is as much an act of judgment as is the original conception, and may be as subject to error. The most common source of difficulty is the misevaluation of current results. When results are unsatisfactory, as we have just pointed out, a reexamination of strategy is called for. At the same time, outstandingly good current results are not necessarily evidence that the strategy is sound. Abnormal upward surges in demand may deceive marginal producers that all is well within their current strategy, until expansion of more efficient competitors wipes out their market share. Extrapolation of present performance into the future, overoptimism and complacence, and underestimation of competitive response and of the time required to accommodate to changes in demand are often by-products of success. Unusually high profits may blind the unwary manager to impending environmental change. His concern for the future can under no circumstances be safely suspended. Conversely, a high-risk strategy that has failed was not necessarily a mistake, so long as the risk was anticipated and the consequences of failure carefully calculated. In fact, a planning problem confronting a number of diversified companies today is how to encourage their divisions to undertake projects where failure can be afforded but where success, if it comes, will be attended by high profits not available in run-of-the-mill, low-risk activities.

Although the possibility of misinterpreting results is by far the commonest obstacle to accurate evaluation of strategy, the criteria previously outlined suggest immediately some additional difficulties. It is as easy to misevaluate corporate resources and the financial requirements of a new move as to misread the environment for future opportunities. To be overresponsive to industry trends may be as dangerous as to ignore them. The correspondence of the company's strategy with current environmental developments and an overreadiness to adapt may obscure the opportunity for a larger share of a declining market or for growth in profits without a parallel growth in total sales. The decision of American Motors not to follow trends toward big cars in the middle 1950s was a strategic alternative running counter to massive current trends in demand.

The intrinsic difficulty of determining and choosing among strategic alternatives leads many companies to do what the rest of the industry is doing rather than to make an independent determination of opportunity and resources. Sometimes the companies of an industry run like sheep all in one direction. The similarity among the strategies, at least in some periods of history, of insurance companies, banks, railroads, and airplane manufacturers may lead one to ask whether strategic decisions were based upon industry convention or upon independent analysis. Whether the similarity of timing, decision, and reaction to competition constitutes independent appraisals of each company's situation, or whether imitation took the place of independent decision is the basis of some wonder. At any rate, the similarity of one company's strategy to that of its competitors does not constitute the assurance of soundness which it might at first suggest.

A strategy may manifest an all-too-clear correspondence with the personal values of the founder, owner, or chief executive. Like a correspondence with dominant trends and the strategic decisions of competitors, this may also be deceptive and unproductive. For example, a personal preference for growth beyond all reasonable expectations may be given undue weight. It should be only one factor among several in any balanced consideration of what is involved in designing strategy. Too little attention to a corporation's actual competence for growth or diversification is the commonest error of all.

It is entirely possible that a strategy may reflect in an exaggerated fashion the values rather than the reasoned decisions of the responsible manager or managers and that imbalance may go undetected. That this may be the case is a reflection of the fact that the entire business community may be dominated by certain beliefs of which one should be wary. A critic of strategy must be at heart enough of a nonconformist to raise questions about generally accepted modes of thought and the conventional thinking which serves as a substitute for original analysis. The timid may not find it prudent to challenge publicly some of the ritual of policy formulation. But even for them it will serve the purposes of criticism to inquire privately into such sacred propositions as the one proclaiming that a company must grow or die or that national planning for energy needs is anathema.

Another canon of management that may engender questionable strategies is the idea that cash funds in excess of reasonable dividend requirements should be reinvested whether in revitalization of a company's traditional activities or in mergers and acquisitions that will diversify products and services. Successful operations, a heretic might observe, sometimes bring riches to a company which lacks the capacity to reemploy them. Yet a decision to return to the owners substantial amounts of capital which the company does not have the competence or desire to put to work is an almost unheard-of development. It is therefore appropriate, particularly in the instance of very successful companies in older and stable industries, to inquire how far strategy reflects a simple desire to put all resources to work rather than a more valid appraisal of investment opportunity in relation to unique corporate strengths. We should not forget to consider an unfashionable, even if ultimately also an untenable, alternative—namely, that to keep an already large worldwide corporation within reasonable bounds, a portion of the assets might well be returned to stockholders for investment in other enterprises.

The identification of opportunity and choice of purpose are such challenging intellectual activities that we should not be surprised to find that persistent problems attend the proper evaluation of strategy. But just as the criteria for evaluation are useful, even if not precise, so the dangers of misevaluation are less menacing if they are recognized. We have noted some inexactness in the concept of strategy, the problems of making resolute deter-

minations in the face of uncertainty, the necessity for
judgment in the evaluation of soundness of strategy, and
the misevaluation into which human error may lead us.
None of these alters the fact that a business enterprise
guided by a clear sense of purpose rationally arrived at
and emotionally ratified by commitment is more likely to
have a successful outcome, in terms of profit and social
good, than a company whose future is left to guesswork
and chance. Conscious strategy does not preclude bril-
liance of improvisation or the welcome consequences of
good fortune. Its cost is principally thought and work for
which it is hard but not impossible to find time.

Chapter three

The company and
its environment:
Relating opportunities
to resources

Determination of a suitable strategy for a company begins in identifying the opportunities and risks in its environment. This chapter is concerned with the identification of a range of strategic alternatives, the narrowing of this range by recognizing the constraints imposed by corporate capability, and the determination of one or more economic strategies at acceptable levels of risk. We shall examine the complexity and variety of the environmental forces which must be considered and the problems in accurately assessing company strengths and weaknesses. Economic strategy will be seen as the match between qualification and opportunity that positions a firm in its product/market environment. We shall attempt in passing to categorize the kinds of economic strategies that can result from the combination of internal capability and external market needs, and to relate these categories to the normal course of corporate development.

THE NATURE OF THE COMPANY'S ENVIRONMENT

The environment of an organization in business, like that of any other organic entity, is the pattern of all the external conditions and influences that affect its life and development. The environmental influences relevant to strategic decision operate in a company's industry, the total business community, its city, its country, and the world. They are technological, economic, physical, social, and political in kind. The corporate strategist is usually at least intuitively aware of these features of the current environment. But in all these categories change is taking place at varying rates—fastest in technology, less rapidly in politics. Change in the environment of business necessitates continuous monitoring of a company's definition of its business, lest it falter, blur, or become obsolete. Since by definition the formulation of strategy is performed with the future in mind, executives who take part in the strategic planning process must be aware of those aspects of their company's environment especially susceptible to the kind of change that will affect their company's future.

Technology.   From the point of view of the corporate strategist, technological developments are not only the fastest unfolding but the most far-reaching in extending or contracting opportunity for an established company. They include the discoveries of science, the impact of related product development, the less dramatic machinery and process improvements, and the progress of automation and data processing. We see generally in technical advance an accelerating rate of change—with new developments arriving before the implications of yesterday's changes can be assimilated. Industries hitherto protected from obsolescence by stable technologies or by the need for huge initial capital investment become more vulnerable more quickly than before to new processes or to cross-industry competition. Periodic lulls do occur to slow the velocity of technical development. Recession, inflation, high interest rates, dislocations in energy costs, divert at times entrepreneurial drive and investment by government and business in research and development to cost reduction and process improvement and to defensive inaction in general. The stubbornness of the major problems still unsolved (for example solar energy, cancer, or automobile emissions) leaves research apparently plateaued from time to time. In view of world competition, however, national policy and corporate drive will not long permit such slowdowns in technical development as seemed to occur as the 1970s came to a close. Science, which does not pause, gives impetus to change not only in technology but also in all other aspects of business activity.

Major areas of technical advance foreseen by students of the management of technology include increased mastery of energy, its conservation and more efficient use, the reorganization of transportation, technical solutions to problems of product life, safety, and serviceability, the further mechanization of logistical functions and the processing of information, alteration in the characteristics of physical and biological materials, and radical developments in controlling air, water, and noise pollution. The primary impact upon established strategies will be increased competition and more rapid obsolescence. The risks dramatized by these technical trends are offset by new business opportunities opened up for companies that are aggressive innovators or adept at technical hitch-hiking. The need intensifies for any company either to engage in technical development or to maintain a technical intelligence capability enabling it to follow quickly new developments pioneered by others.

Ecology. It used to be possible to take for granted the physical characteristics of the environment and find them favorable to industrial development. Plant sites were chosen using criteria like availability of process and cooling water, accessibility to various forms of transportation, and stability of soil conditions. With the increase in sensitivity to the impact on the physical environment of all industrial activity, it becomes essential, often to comply with law, to consider how planned expansion and even continued operation under changing standards will affect and be perceived to affect the air, water, traffic density, and quality of life generally of any area which a company would like to enter. The tradeoff between economic production and preservation or improvement of the ecological status quo has been dramatically revealed in the use of plentiful high-sulfur coal in the generation of electric power in place of imported oil. In specific instances predictions involving high risk must be made about how such tradeoffs will be resolved in the ebb and flow of public opinion.

Economics.   Because business is more accustomed to monitoring economic trends than those in other spheres, it is less likely to be taken by surprise by such massive developments as the internationalization of competition, the return of China and Russia to trade with the West, the slower than projected development of the Third World countries, the Americanization of demand and culture in the developing countries and the resulting backlash of nationalism, the increased importance of the large multinational corporations and the consequences of host-country hostility, the recurrence of recession, and the persistence of inflation in all phases of the business cycle. The consequences of world economic trends need to be monitored in much greater detail for any one industry or company.

Industry.   Although the industry environment is the one most company strategists believe they know most about, the opportunities and risks that reside there are often blurred by familiarity and the uncritical acceptance of the established relative position of competitors.

Michael Porter,[1] in an effort to develop strategically useful analysis of the structure of industries, has decided that
the nature of competition in an industry and its profit potential are affected by certain structural determinants—
the threat of entry by new firms, the relative power of
suppliers and customers, and the development of substitute products by other industries. Whether an industry is
fragmented, emerging, maturing, or declining affects
strategic opportunity as much as whether it produces
basic commodities or products reflecting rapid technological change.

A close look at any industry will reveal its strategic
dimensions and the strategic groups consisting of companies that have made similar decisions about these dimensions. Strategy formulation in this view becomes a
decision of which strategic group to compete in, without
precluding the preservation of competitive advantage
within the group. Reading market signals consciously or
unconsciously offered by competitors gives clues to competitors' motives, goals, internal situations, and intentions. The strategic significance of changes going on in
industry structure as it evolves around the jockeying of
competitors for position should be determined in the
search for opportunity in the total environment of the firm.

Society. Social developments of which strategists
keep aware include such influential forces as the quest for
equality for minority groups, the demand of women for
opportunity and recognition, the changing patterns of
work and leisure, the effects of urbanization upon the individual, family, and neighborhood, the rise of crime, the

---

[1]Michael E. Porter, *Competitive Strategy: Techniques for Analyzing Industries and Competitors* (New York: Free Press, 1980). See also his "How Competitive Forces Shape Strategy," *Harvard Business Review*, March–April 1979,
pp. 137–45.

decline of conventional morality, and the changing composition of world population.

Politics. The political forces important to the business firm are similarly extensive and complex—the changing relations between communist and noncommunist countries (East and West) and between the prosperous and poor countries (North and South), the relation between private enterprise and government, between workers and management, the impact of national planning on corporate planning, and the rise of what George Lodge calls the communitarian ideology.[2] The 1980s will see greater attention by business to government as regulation restricts and channels initiative. The amount of time those who serve as chief strategic officers of sizable corporations must spend in considering jointly in legislative committees proposals for corporate governance increases steadily. Such exposure should equip corporate leadership to anticipate public concern and take it into account in making strategic decisions.

Although it is not possible to know or spell out here the significance of such technical, economic, social, and political trends, and possibilities for the strategist of a given business or company, some simple things are clear. Changing values will lead to different expectations of the role business should perform. Business will be expected to perform its mission not only with economy in the use of energy but with sensitivity to the ecological environment. Organizations in all walks of life will be called upon to be more explicit about their goals and to meet the needs and aspirations (for example, for education) of their membership.

---

[2]George C. Lodge,*The New American Ideology* (New York: Alfred A. Knopf, Inc., 1975).

In any case, change threatens all established strategies. We know that a thriving company—itself a living system—is bound up in a variety of interrelationships with larger systems comprising its technological, economic, ecological, social, and political environment. If environmental developments are destroying and creating business opportunities, advance notice of specific instances relevant to a single company is essential to intelligent planning. Risk and opportunity in the last quarter of the 20th century require of executives a keen interest in what is going on outside their companies. More than that, a practical means of tracking developments promising good or ill, and profit or loss, needs to be devised.

TRACKING THE CHANGING ENVIRONMENT

Unfortunately the development of knowledge in a flourishing business civilization has produced no easy methodology for continuous surveillance of the trends in the environment of central importance to a firm of ordinary capabilities. Predictive theories of special disciplines such as economics, sociology, psychology, and anthropology do not produce comprehensive appraisal readily applicable to long-range corporate strategic decision. At the same time many techniques do exist to deal with parts of the problem—economic and technological forecasting, detailed demographic projections, geological estimates of raw material reserves, national and international statistics in which trends may be discerned. More information about the environment is available than is commonly used.

John D. Glover has developed an approach to the total

environment of a business firm as an ecological system.[3]
His framework consists of four subsystems (the immediate total community of a company, the culture in which
it operates, the flow of goods and services being produced
or consumed, the natural and manmade physical setting).
For each of these categories an enormous amount of data
is available, with projections of future movement.
Schemes such as Glover's provide the means for planning
staffs to reduce to rational analysis what is now practicing managers' intuitive and fragmentary vision of the developing forces offering opportunity to their firms and
taking it away.

Further study of the problem of strategic information
would take you to Aguilar's research in how managers in
the chemical industry obtained strategic information
about environmental change.[4] Aguilar found that even in
this technically sensitive industry, few firms attempted
any systematic means for gathering and evaluating such
information. Publications provided only about 20 percent
of the information from all sources, with current market
and competitive information from personal sources
dominating the total input of information. Internally
generated information comprised only 9 percent of the total, and more information received was unsolicited than
solicited. (Interestingly enough, very few people in subordinate positions felt they were getting useful strategic
information from their superiors.)

Aguilar's findings were corroborated by Robert Col-

---

[3]Most of this work is unpublished, but Glover's approach is summarized in
"Strategic Decision-Making: Planning, Manning, Organization," in John D.
Glover and Gerald A. Simon, *Chief Executives' Handbook* (Homewood, Ill.:
Dow Jones-Irwin, 1976), pp. 423–41. © 1976 by Dow Jones-Irwin, Inc.

[4]Frank J. Aguilar, *Scanning the Business Environment* (New York: The
Macmillan Company, 1967).

lings' study of investment firms.[5] The obvious moral of these studies is that the process of obtaining strategic information is far from being systematic, complete, or even really informative about anything except current developments, at least in these industries. These researchers show that it is possible to organize better the gathering and integrating of environmental data through such means as bringing miscellaneous scanning activities together and communicating available information internally.

We should not be carried away by this possibility, for limitations of time, interest, and willpower will no doubt continue to leave word of mouth, coalescing occasionally to establish conventional wisdom, the dominant mode of communication among senior managers, who are often accused of thinking very much alike. This human tendency occasionally presents opportunities for the strategists who out of originality or perversity decide that the opposite of what they hear is the truth.

Certain large companies organize a disciplined inquiry to undergird the assumptions of their leaders about the future. General Electric has maintained for years a Business Environment Section at its corporate headquarters and prepares reports on predicted changes for use by its divisions. Consulting firms, future-oriented research organizations, and associations of planners provide guidance for looking ahead. The sense of futility experienced by executives in the face of complexity is reduced when they begin the task by defining their strategy and the most likely strategic alternatives they will be debating in the foreseeable future. Decision on direction spotlights the relevant environment. You cannot know everything, but

[5]Robert Collings, "Scanning the Environment for Strategic Information" (unpublished doctoral thesis, Harvard Business School).

if you are thinking of going into the furniture business in Nebraska you will not be immoderately concerned about the rate of family formation in Japan. Clarification of present strategy and the few new alternatives it suggests narrows sharply the range of necessary information and destroys the excuse that there is too much to know.

IDENTIFICATION OF OPPORTUNITIES AND RISKS

For the firm that has not determined what its strategy dictates it needs to know or has not embarked upon the systematic surveillance of environmental change, a few simple questions kept constantly in mind will highlight changing opportunity and risk. In examining your own company or one you are interested in, these questions should lead to an estimate of opportunity and danger in the present and predicted company setting.

1. *What are the essential economic, technical, and physical characteristics of the industry in which the company participates?*

Whether these are in flux or not, such characteristics may define the restrictions and opportunities confronting the individual company, and will certainly suggest strategy for it. For example, knowledge that the cement industry requires high investment in plant, proximity to a certain combination of raw materials, a relatively small labor force, and enormous fuel and transportation costs suggests where to look for new plant sites and what will constitute competitive advantage and disadvantage. The nature of its product may suggest for a given company the wisdom of developing efficient pipeline and truck transportation and cheaper energy sources rather than engaging in extensive research to achieve product differentiation or aggressive price competition to increase its market share.

2. What trends suggesting future change in economic and technical characteristics are apparent?

Changes in demand for the product of one industry in competition with the products of another, and changes in the product itself, occurring as a result of research and development, affect the chance for growth. For example, the glass container industry's development years ago of strong, light, disposable bottles and more recently combinations of glass and plastic recouped part of the market lost by glass to the metal container. The need for the glass industry to engage in this development effort was made apparent by the observable success of the metal beer can. Similarly, the easy-opening metal container suggested the need for an easily removable bottle cap. The physical characteristics of any product can be examined against the master trend toward simplicity, convenience, and serviceability in consumer goods and against competitive innovations. Both the glass bottle and the metal container face increasingly effective attack by environmentalists, who constitute a noneconomic and nontechnical force to be reckoned with. Container industries should have begun long since, for example, to develop logistical solutions to the legislatively mandated returnable bottle and can.

3. What is the nature of competition both within the industry and across industries?

A small rubber company, in an industry led by Uniroyal, Goodyear, Goodrich, and Firestone, will not, under the economic condition of overcapacity, elect to provide the automobile business with original tires for new cars. The structure of competition, quite apart from the resources of the firm, may suggest that a relatively

small firm should seek out a niche of relatively small attraction to the majors, and concentrate its powers on that
limited segment of the market.

Present and developing competition usually extends,
of course, beyond the industry in which a company finds
itself. For example, the competition for the cement industry from producers of asphalt road-building materials is
as important as that from other cement producers.

4.   *What are the requirements for success in competition in the company's industry?*

In every industry some critical tasks must be performed
particularly well to ensure survival. In the ladies' belt and
handbag business style and design are critical, but so
(less obviously) are relationships with department store
buyers. In the computer business, a sales force able to
diagnose customer requirements for information systems,
to design a suitable system, and to equip a customer to
use it is more important than the circuitry of hardware.

Although the question of what tasks are most critical
may be chiefly useful as a means of identifying risks or
possible causes of failure, it may also suggest opportunity. Imagination in perceiving new requirements for success under changing conditions, when production-ori-
ented competitors have not done so, can give a company
leadership position. For example, opportunity for a local
radio station and the strategy it needed to follow changed
sharply with the rise of television, and those who first
diagnosed the new requirements paid much less for sta-
tions than was later necessary.

5.   *Given the technical, economic, social, and political developments that most directly apply, what is the
range of strategy available to any company in this industry?*

The force of this question is obvious in the drug industry. The speed and direction of pharmaceutical research, the structure of the industry, the characteristics of worldwide demand, the different and changing ideas about how adequate medical care should be made available to the world's population, the concern about price, and the nature of government regulation suggest constraints within which a range of opportunity is still vividly clear. Similarly, in a more stable industry, there is always a choice. To determine its limits, an examination of environmental characteristics and developments is essential.

OPPORTUNITY AS A DETERMINANT OF STRATEGY

Awareness of the environment is not a special project to be undertaken only when warning of change becomes deafening; it is a continuing requirement for informed choice of purpose. Planned exploitation of changing opportunity ordinarily follows a predictable course which provides increasing awareness of areas to which a company's capabilities may be profitably extended. A useful way to perceive the normal course of development is to use Bruce Scott's stages referred to briefly above.

The manufacturer of a single product (Stage I) sold within a clearly defined geographical area to meet a known demand finds it relatively easy to identify opportunity and risk. As an enterprise develops a degree of complexity requiring functional division or management decision, it encounters as an integrated Stage II company a number of strategic alternatives in its market environments which the Stage I proprietor is too hard pressed to notice and almost too overcommitted to consider. Finally, Stage III companies, deployed along the full range of diversification, find even a greater number of possibilities for serving a market profitably than the resources they possess or have in sight will support. The more one finds out what might be done, the harder it is to make the final choice.

The diversified Stage III company has another problem different from that of trying to make the best choice among many. If it has divisionalized its operations and strategies, as sooner or later in the course of diversification it must, then divisional opportunities come into competition with each other. Strategy formulation and environmental surveillance become organization processes.

The corporate management normally will wish to invest profits not distributed to stockholders in those opportunities that will produce the greatest return to the corporation. If need be, corporate management, after portfolio analysis, will be willing to let an individual division decline if its future looks less attractive than that of others. The division on the other hand will wish to protect its own market position, ward off adverse development, prolong its own existence, and provide for its growth. The division manager, who is not rewarded for failures, may program projects of safe but usually not dramatic prospects. The claims regarding projected return on investment, which are submitted in all honesty as the divisional estimate of future opportunity, can be assumed to be biased by the division's regard for its own interest and the manager's awareness of measurement.

The corporate management cannot be expected to be able to make independent judgments about all the proposals for growth which are submitted by all the divisions. On the other hand, all divisions cannot be given their heads, if the corporation's needs for present profit are to be met and if funds for reinvestment are limited. In any case, the greatest knowledge about the opportunities for a given technology and set of markets should be found at the divisional level.[6]

The strategic dilemma of a conglomerate world enterprise is the most complex in the full range of policy decisions. When the variety of what must be known cannot be reduced by a sharply focused strategy to the capacity of a single mind and when the range of a company's activities spans many industries and technologies, the problems of formulating a coherent strategy begin to get out of hand. Here strategy must become a managed process rather than the decision of the chief executive officer and his immediate associates. Bower and Prahalad have shown in important research how the context of decision can be controlled by the top management group and how power can be distributed through a hierarchy to influence the kind of strategic decision that will survive in the system.[7] The process of strategic decision can, like complex operations, be organized in such a way as to provide appropriate complementary roles for decentralization and control.

To conceive of a new development in response to market information and prediction of the future is a creative act. To commit resources to it only on the basis of projected return and the estimate of probability constituting risk of failure is foolhardy. More than economic

---

[6]See Norman Berg, "Strategic Planning in Conglomerate Companies," *Harvard Business Review*, May–June 1965, pp. 79–92.

[7]Joseph L. Bower, *Managing the Resource Allocation Process* (Boston: Division of Research, Harvard Business School, 1970); and C. K. Prahalad, "The Strategic Process in a Multinational Corporation" (unpublished doctoral thesis, Harvard Business School, 1975), partially summarized in "Strategic Choices in Diversified MNCs," *Harvard Business Review*, July–August 1976, pp. 67–78.

analysis of potential return is required for decision, for economic opportunity abounds, far beyond the ability to capture it. That much money might be made in a new field or growth industry does not mean that a company with abilities developed in a different field is going to make it. We turn now to the critical factors that for an individual company make one opportunity better than another.

IDENTIFYING CORPORATE COMPETENCE AND RESOURCES

The first step in validating a tentative choice among several opportunities is to determine whether the organization has the capacity to prosecute it successfully. The capability of an organization is its demonstrated and potential ability to accomplish, against the opposition of circumstance or competition, whatever it sets out to do. Every organization has actual and potential strengths and weaknesses. Since it is prudent in formulating strategy to extend or maximize the one and contain or minimize the other, it is important to try to determine what they are and to distinguish one from the other.

It is just as possible, though much more difficult, for a company to know its own strengths and limitations as it is to maintain a workable surveillance of its changing environment. Subjectivity, lack of confidence, and unwillingness to face reality may make it hard for organizations as well as for individuals to know themselves. But just as it is essential, though difficult, that a maturing person achieve reasonable self-awareness, so an organization can identify approximately its central strength and critical vulnerability.

Howard H. Stevenson has made the first formal study of management practice in defining corporate strengths and weaknesses as part of the strategic planning process.[8] He looked at five aspects of the process: (1) the attributes of the company which its managers examined, (2) the organizational scope of the strengths and weaknesses identified, (3) the measurement employed in the process of definition, (4) the criteria for telling a strength from a weakness, and (5) the sources of relevant information. As might be expected, the process Stevenson was looking at was imperfectly and variously practiced in the half dozen companies he studied. He found that the problems of definition of corporate strengths and weaknesses, very different from those of other planning processes, center mostly upon a general lack of agreement on suitable definition, criteria, and information. For an art that has hardly made a beginning, Stevenson's most important conclusion is that the attempt to define strengths and weaknesses is more useful than the usual final product of the process.

Stevenson's exploratory study in no way diminishes the importance of trying to appraise organization capability. It protects against oversimplification. The absence of criteria and measures, the disinclination for appraising competence except in relation to specific problems, the uncertainty about what is meant by "strength" and "weakness," and the reluctance to imply criticism of individuals or organizational subunits—all these hampered his study but illuminated the problem. Much of what is intuitive in this process is yet to be identified. Essential to

---

[8]Howard H. Stevenson, "Defining Corporate Strengths and Weaknesses: An Exploratory Study" (an unpublished doctoral thesis deposited in Baker Library, Harvard Business School, 1969). For a published summary article of the same title, see Sloan Management Review, Spring 1976.

effective membership in an organization is the capacity as an individual to see through the loyalty he or she feels to its objectively ascertainable capabilities.

To make an effective contribution to strategic planning, the key attributes to be appraised should be identified and consistent criteria established for judging them. If attention is directed to strategies, policy commitments, and past practices in the context of discrepancy between organization goals and attainment, an outcome useful to an individual manager's strategic planning is possible. The assessment of strengths and weaknesses associated with the attainment of specific objectives becomes in Stevenson's words a "key link in a feedback loop" which allows managers to learn from the success or failures of the policies they institute.

Although this study does not find or establish a systematic way of developing or using such knowledge, members of organizations develop judgments about what the company can do particularly well—its core of competence. If consensus can be reached about this capability, no matter how subjectively arrived at, its application to identified opportunity can be estimated.

Sources of capabilities.   The powers of a company constituting a resource for growth and diversification accrue primarily from experience in making and marketing a product line or providing a service. They inhere as well in (1) the developing strengths and weaknesses of the individuals comprising the organization, (2) the degree to which individual capability is effectively applied to the common task, and (3) the quality of coordination of individual and group effort.

The experience gained through successful execution of a strategy centered upon one goal may unexpectedly develop capabilities which could be applied to different ends. Whether they should be so applied is another question. For example, a manufacturer of salt can strengthen his competitive position by offering his customers salt-dispensing equipment. If, in the course of making engineering improvements in this equipment, a new solenoid principle is perfected that has application to many industrial switching problems, should this patentable and marketable innovation be exploited? The answer would turn not only on whether economic analysis of the opportunity shows this to be a durable and profitable possibility, but also on whether the organization can muster the financial, manufacturing, and marketing strength to exploit the discovery and live with its success. The former question is likely to have a more positive answer than the latter. In this connection, it seems important to remember that individual and unsupported flashes of strength are not as dependable as the gradually accumulated product and market-related fruits of experience.

Even where competence to exploit an opportunity is nurtured by experience in related fields, the level of that competence may be too low for any great reliance to be placed upon it. Thus a chain of children's clothing stores might well acquire the administrative, merchandising, buying, and selling skills that would permit it to add departments in women's wear. Similarly, a sales force effective in distributing typewriters might gain proficiency in selling office machinery and supplies. But even here it would be well to ask what *distinctive* ability these companies could bring to the retailing of soft goods or office equipment to attract customers away from a plethora of competitors.

Identifying strengths. The distinctive competence of an organization is more than what it can do; it is what it can do particularly well. To identify the less obvious or by-product strengths of an organization that may well be transferable to some more profitable new opportunity, one might well begin by examining the organization's current product line and by defining the functions it serves in its markets. Almost any important consumer product has functions which are related to others into which a qualified company might move. The typewriter, for example, is more than the simple machine for mechanizing handwriting that it once appeared to be when looked at only from the point of view of its designer and manufacturer. Closely analyzed from the point of view of the potential user, the typewriter is found to contribute to a broad range of information processing functions. Any one of these might have suggested an area to be exploited by a typewriter manufacturer. Tacitly defining a typewriter as a replacement for a fountain pen as a writing instrument rather than as an input-output device for word processing is the explanation provided by hindsight for the failure of the old-line typewriter companies to develop before IBM did the electric typewriter and the computer-related input-output devices it made possible. The definition of product which would lead to identification of transferable skills must be expressed in terms of the market needs it may fill rather than the engineering specifications to which it conforms.

Besides looking at the uses or functions to which present products contribute, the would-be diversifier might profitably identify the skills that underlie whatever success has been achieved. The qualifications of an organization efficient at performing its long-accustomed tasks come to be taken for granted and considered humdrum, like the steady provision of first-class service. The insight required to identify the essential strength justifying new ventures does not come naturally. Its cultivation can probably be helped by recognition of the need for analysis. In any case, we should look beyond the company's capacity to invent new products. Product leadership is not possible for a majority of companies, so it is fortunate that patentable new products are not the only major highway to new opportunities. Other avenues include new marketing services, new methods of distribution, new values in quality-price combinations, and creative merchandising. The effort to find or to create a competence that is truly distinctive may hold the real key to a company's success or even to its future development. For example, the ability of a cement manufacturer to run a truck fleet more effectively than its competitors may constitute one of its principal competitive strengths in selling an undifferentiated product.

Matching opportunity and competence. The way to narrow the range of alternatives, made extensive by imaginative identification of new possibilities, is to match opportunity to competence, once each has been accurately identified and its future significance estimated. It is this combination which establishes a company's economic mission and its position in its environment. The combination is designed to minimize organizational weakness and to maximize strength. In every case, risk attends it. And when opportunity seems to outrun present distinctive competence, the willingness to gamble that the latter can be built up to the required level is almost indispensable to a strategy that challenges the organization and the people in it. Figure 2 diagrams the matching of opportunity and resources that results in an economic strategy.

Before we leave the creative act of putting together a company's unique internal capability and opportunity

FIGURE 2: SCHEMATIC DEVELOPMENT OF ECONOMIC STRATEGY

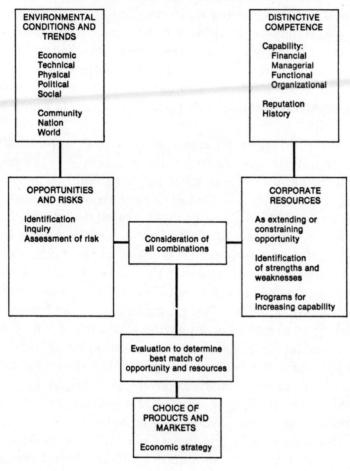

evolving in the external world, we should note that—
aside from distinctive competence—the principal resources found in any company are money and people—
technical and managerial people. At an advanced stage of
economic development, money seems less a problem
than technical competence, and the latter less critical

than managerial ability. Do not assume that managerial capacity can rise to any occasion. The diversification of American industry is marked by hundreds of instances in which a company strong in one endeavor lacked the ability to manage an enterprise requiring different skills. The right to make handsome profits over a long period must be earned. Opportunism without competence is a path to fairyland.

Besides equating an appraisal of market opportunity and organizational capability, the decision to make and market a particular product or service should be accompanied by an identification of the nature of the business and the kind of company its management desires. Such a guiding concept is a product of many considerations, including the managers' personal values. As such, this concept will change more slowly than other aspects of the organization, and it will give coherence to all the variety of company activities. For example, a president who is determined to make his or her firm into a worldwide producer and fabricator of a basic metal, through policies differentiating it from the industry leader, will not be distracted by excess capacity in developed markets, by low metal prices, and by cutthroat competition in certain markets. Such a firm would not be sidetracked into acquiring, for example, the Pepsi-Cola franchise in Africa, even if this business promised to yield a good profit. (That such a firm should have an experimental division exploring offshoot technology is, however, entirely appropriate.)

Uniqueness of strategy. In each company, the way in which distinctive competence, organizational resources, and organizational values are combined is or should be unique. Differences among companies are as numerous as differences among individuals. The combinations of opportunity to which distinctive competences, resources, and values may be applied are equally extensive. Generalizing about how to make an effective match is less rewarding than working at it. The effort is a highly stimulating and challenging exercise. The outcome will be unique for each company and each situation.

APPLICATION TO SITUATIONS

Because all these observations do not bear fruit until their potency is tested in actual company situations, you should be thinking by now about the strategy of the organization you are managing or know best. Against the general need to articulate and appraise its strategy and with the aim of generating alternatives for its improvement, these questions should focus attention upon the usefulness to you of what you have just been reading.

What really is our product? What functions does it serve? To what additional functions might it be extended or adapted?

What is happening to the market for our products? Is it expanding or contracting? Why?

What are our company's major strengths and weaknesses? From what sources do these arise?

Do we have a distinctive or core competence? If so, to what new activities can it be applied?

What is the structure of our industry? Who are its leaders? What are its subgroups of companies? Where do we fit? How is the industry changing?

What are our principal competitors' major strengths and weaknesses? Are they imitating us or we them? What comparative advantage over our competitors can we exploit?

What is our strategy? Is the combination of product and market an optimum economic strategy? Is the central nature of our business clear enough to provide us with a criterion for product diversification?

What, if any, better combinations of market opportunities and distinctive competence can our company effect, within a range of reasonable risk?

These questions may prove helpful in the task of designing or validating an economic strategy. However, they are never wholly sufficient, for the strategic decision is never wholly economic in character. Corporate strategy is much more than a series of product-market decisions.

Chapter four

The company and its strategists: Relating corporate strategy to personal values

Up to this point we have argued that a concept of purpose and a sense of direction strengthen a company's ability to survive in changing circumstances. We have seen, to be sure, the difficulties of understanding clearly both a company's circumstances and its strengths and weaknesses. The action implied by these difficulties has been an objective and alert surveillance of the environment for threats and opportunities and a detached appraisal of organizational characteristics in order to identify distinctive competence. We have considered the suitable combination of a company's strengths and its opportunities to be a logical exercise characterized by perhaps not precise but reasoned, well-informed choices of alternatives assuring the highest possible profit. We have been examining the changing relationship of company and environment almost as if a purely economic strategy, uncontaminated by the personality or goals of the decision maker, were possible.

STRATEGY AS PROJECTION OF PREFERENCE

We must acknowledge at this point that there is no way to divorce the decision determining the most sensible economic strategy for a company from the personal values of those who make the choice. Executives in charge of company destinies do not look exclusively at what a company might do and can do. In apparent disregard of the second of these considerations, they sometimes seem heavily influenced by what they personally *want* to do.

74

We are ourselves not aware of how much desire affects our own choice of alternatives, but we can see it in others. Note, for example, George Romney's dramatic promotion of economically sensible transportation and the small car in the early days of American Motors and his subsequent repayment of all debt, in place of investment through research in the development of variations in the small car which might have retained leadership in an important segment of the market. Almost certainly we see reflected here the higher value Romney placed on economy than on consumer preferences, on liquidity over debt, and other values derived more from his character and upbringing than from an objective monitoring of the best course for American Motors to follow.

Frank Farwell came from IBM to the presidency of Underwood in 1955, it has been said, saying that he would be damned if he would spend his life peddling adding machines and typewriters. This aversion may explain why Underwood plunged into the computer business without the technical, financial, or marketing resources necessary to succeed in it. Similarly, when Adriano Olivetti purchased control of Underwood after three days of hurried negotiations, he may well have been moved by his childhood memory of visiting Hartford and by the respect for the world's once leading manufacturer of typewriters that led his father to erect in Ivrea a replica of the red-brick, five-story Hartford plant.[1] That he wanted to purchase Underwood so badly may explain

---

[1] See "Underwood-Olivetti (AR)," Edmund P. Learned, C. Roland Christensen, Kenneth R. Andrews, and William D. Guth, Business Policy: Text and Cases, original edition (Homewood, Ill.: Richard D. Irwin, 1965), p. 212. This case is also in the Intercollegiate Case Clearing House, (Boston, 02163) No. 9–312–017.

why he and his associates did not find out how danger-
ously it had decayed and how near bankruptcy it had
been brought.

The three presidents of J. I. Case in the years 1953 to
1963 seem to have been displaying their own tempera-
ments as they wracked the company with alternatives of
expansionism and contraction far beyond the needs of response to a cyclical industry environment.[2] In all these
cases, the actions taken can be rationalized so as not to
seem quite so personal as I have suggested they are.

THE INEVITABILITY OF VALUES

We will be able to understand the strategic decision
better if we admit rather than resist the dimension of
preference. If we think back over the discussions of earlier cases in this book, the strategies we recommended for
the companies probably reflected what we would have
wanted to do had we been in charge of those companies.
We told ourselves or assumed that our personal inclinations harmonized with the optimum combination of
economic opportunity and company capability. The professional manager in a large company, drilled in analytical technique and the use of staff trained to subordinate
value-laden assumptions to tables of numbers, may often
prefer the optimal economic strategy because of its very
suitability. Certain entrepreneurs, whose energy and personal drives far outweigh their formal training and self-
awareness, set their course in directions not necessarily
supported by logical appraisal. Such disparity appears

---

[2] "J. I. Case Company," Learned et al., *Business Policy*, pp. 82–102. This
case is also in the Intercollegiate Case Clearing House, No. 9–309–270.

most frequently in small privately held concerns, or in companies built by successful and self-confident owner-managers. The phenomenon we are discussing, however, may appear in any company, especially if it is large, or in its divisions.

Our problem now can be very simply stated. In examining the alternatives available to a company, we must henceforth take into consideration the preferences of the chief executive. Furthermore, we must also be concerned with the values of other key managers who must either contribute to or assent to the strategy if it is to be effective. We therefore have two kinds of reconciliation to consider—first, the divergence between the chief executive's preference and the strategic choice which seems most economically defensible, and second, the conflict among several sets of managerial personal values which must be reconciled not only with an economic strategy but with each other.

Thus, when Mr. Edgar Villchur, inventor of the acoustic suspension loudspeaker, founded Acoustic Research, Inc.,[3] in 1954, he institutionalized a desire to bring high fidelity sound to the mass market at the lowest possible cost. He licensed his competitors freely and finally gave up his original patent rights altogether. He kept not only his prices but his dealer margins low, maintained for a considerable time a primitive production facility and an organization of friends rather than managers, and went to great lengths to make the company a good place to work, sharing with employees the company's success. The company was dominated by Mr. Villchur's desire to have a small organization characterized by academic, scientific, and intellectual rather than "commercial" values.

---

[3]"Acoustic Research, Inc.," Learned et al., *Business Policy*, pp. 466–519. This case is in the Intercollegiate Case Clearing House, No. 9–312–020.

Product development was driven by some of these values away from the acoustical technology which Mr. Villchur's personal competence would have suggested into development of record players, amplifiers, and tuners which were to offer less in superiority over competitive products than did his speakers. Again, these were priced far below what might have been possible.

Mr. Abraham Hoffman, for years vice president and treasurer, had the task of trying to overcome his superior's reluctance to advertise, to admit the validity of the marketing function, and to run the business as a profitable enterprise. That the company had succeeded in at long last developing and producing a music system of great value in relation to its cost and in winning the respect of the high fidelity listener market does not alter the fact that the first determination of strategy came more from Mr. Villchur's antibusiness values than from an analytical balancing of opportunity and distinctive competence. The latter would have led, with perhaps much greater growth and profitability, into acoustical systems, public address equipment, long-distance communications, hearing aids, noise suppression, and the like—all areas in which technical improvement in the quality of available sound is much needed.

We must remember, however, that it is out of Mr. Villchur's determination and goals that his company came into being in the first place. The extraordinary accomplishments of an antimarketing company in the marketplace are directly traceable to the determination to innovate in quality and price. The reconciliation between Mr. Villchur's values and Mr. Hoffman's more business-oriented determination to manage the company's growth more objectively occurred only when the company was sold to Teledyne, Mr. Villchur retired to his laboratory, and Mr. Hoffman became president. The quality achievements of this firm have been rewarded, but the economic potential of its strategy was for years unrealized.

We should in all realism admit that the personal desires, aspirations, and needs of the senior managers of a company actually do play an influential role in the determination of strategy. Against those who are offended by this idea either for its departure from the stereotype of single-minded economic man or for its implicit violation of responsibilities to the shareholder, we would argue that we must accept not only the inevitability but the desirability of this intervention. If we begin by saying that all strategic decisions must fall within the very broad limits of the manager's fiduciary responsibility to the owners of the business and perhaps to others in the management group, then we may proceed legitimately to the idea that what a manager wants to do is not out of order. The conflict which often arises between what general managers want to do and what the dictates of economic strategy suggest they ought to do is best not denied or condemned. It should be accepted as a matter of course. In the study of organization behavior, we have long since concluded that the personal needs of the hourly worker must be taken seriously and at least partially satisfied as a means of securing the productive effort for which wages are paid. It should, then, come as no surprise to us that the president of the corporation also arrives at his work with his own needs and values, to say nothing of his relatively greater power to see that they are taken into account.

RECONCILING DIVERGENT VALUES

If we accept the inevitability of personal values in the

strategic decision governing the character and course of a corporation, then we must turn to the skills required to reconcile the optimal economic strategy with the personal preferences of the executives of the company. There is no reason why a better balance could not have been struck in Acoustic Research, without sacrifice to the genius of the founder or the quality of life in his company. It is first necessary to penetrate conventional rationalization and reticence to determine what these preferences are. For without this revelation, strategic proposals stemming from different unstated values come into conflict. This conflict cannot be reconciled by talking in terms of environmental data and corporate resources. The hidden agenda of corporate policy debates makes them endless and explains why so many companies do not have explicit, forthright, and usefully focused strategies.

To many caught up in the unresolved strategic questions in their own organizations, it seems futile even to attempt to reconcile a strategic alternative dictated by personal preference with other alternatives oriented toward capitalizing on opportunity to the greatest possible extent. In actuality, however, this additional complication poses fewer difficulties than at first appear. The analysis of opportunity and the appraisal of resources themselves often lead in different directions. To compose three, rather than two, divergent sets of considerations into a single pattern may increase the complexity of the task, but the integrating process is still the same. We can look for the dominant consideration and treat the others as constraints; we can probe the elements in conflict for the possibilities of reinterpretation or adjustment. We are not building a wall of irregular stone so much as balancing a mobile of elements, the motion of which is adjustable to the motion of the entire mobile.

As we have seen, external developments can be affected by company action and company resources, and internal competence can be developed. If worst comes to worst, it is better for a person to separate from a management whose values he or she does not share than to pretend agreement or to wonder why others think as they do. Howard Head, whose passionate dedication to the metal ski not only produced a most successful business, but delayed unnecessarily its entry into plastic skis, has realistically retired from his now diversified business and has sold his holdings. It is not necessary, however, for all members of management to think alike or to have the same personal values, so long as strategic decision is not delayed or rendered ineffective by these known and accepted differences. Large gains are possible simply by raising the strategic issues for discussion by top management, by admitting the legitimacy of different preferences, and by exploring how superficial or fundamental the differences are.

MODIFICATION OF VALUES

The question whether values can actually be changed during the reconciliation process is somewhat less clear. A value is a view of life and a judgment of what is desirable that is very much a part of a person's personality and a group's morale. From parents, teachers, and peers, we are told by psychologists, we acquire basic values, which change somewhat with acquired knowledge, analytical ability, and self-awareness, but remain a stable feature of personality.[4] Nonetheless the preference attached to goals

---

[4]See for example W. D. Guth and Renato Tagiuri: "Personal Values and Corporate Strategy," *Harvard Business Review*, September–October 1965, pp. 123–32.

in concrete circumstances is not beyond influence. The physicist who leaves the university to work in a profit-making company because of a combined fondness for his work and for material comfort, may ask to continue to do pure rather than applied research, but he presumably does not want his company to go bankrupt. The conflict in values is to some degree negotiable, once the reluctance to expose hidden agendas is overcome. Retaining the value orientation of the scientist, the ambivalent physicist might assent to a strategic alternative stressing product development rather than original investigation, at least for a specified time until the attainment of adequate profit makes longer range research feasible.

AWARENESS OF VALUES

Our interest in the role of personal values in strategic formulations should not be confined to assessing the influence of other people's values. Despite the well-known problems of introspection, we can probably do more to understand the relation of our own values to our choice of purpose than we can to change the values of others. Awareness that our own preference for an alternative opposed by another stems from values as much as from rational estimates of economic opportunity may have important consequences. First, it may make us more tolerant and less indignant when we perceive this relationship between recommendations and values in the formulations of others. Second, it will force us to consider how important it really is to us to maintain a particular value in making a particular decision. Third, it may give us insight with which to identify our biases and thus pave the way for a more objective assessment of all the strategic alternatives that are available. These consequences of self-examination will not end conflict, but they will at least prevent its unnecessary prolongation.

The object of this self-examination is not necessarily to endow us with the ability to persuade others to accept the strategic recommendations we consider best: it is to acquire insight into the problems of determining purpose and skill in the process of resolving them. Individuals inquiring into their own values for the purpose of understanding their own positions in policy debates can continue to assess their own personal opportunities, strengths and weaknesses, and basic values by means of the procedures outlined here. For a personal strategy, analytically considered and consciously developed, may be as useful to an individual as a corporate strategy is to a business institution. The effort, conducted by each individual, to formulate personal purpose might well accompany his or her contributions to organizational purpose. If the encounter leads to a clarification of the purposes one seeks, the values one holds, and the alternatives available, the attempt to make personal use of the concept of strategy will prove extremely worthwhile.

Introducing personal preference forces us to deal with the possibility that the strategic decision we prefer (identified after the most nearly objective analysis of opportunity and resources we are capable of) is not acceptable to other executives with different values. Their acceptance of the strategy is necessary to its successful implementation. In diagnosing this conflict, we try to identify the values implicit in our own choice. As we look at the gap between the strategy which follows from our own values and that which would be appropriate to the values of our associates, we look to see whether the difference is fundamental or superficial. Then we look to see how the

strategy we believe best matches opportunity and resources can be adapted to accommodate the values of
those who will implement it. Reconciliation of the three
principal determinants of strategy which we have so far
considered is often made possible by adjustment of any or
all of the determinants.

The role of self-examination in coming to terms with a
conflict in values over an important strategic determination is not to turn all strategic decisions into outcomes of
consensus. Some organizations are run by persons who
are leaders in the sense that they have power and are not
afraid to use it. It is true that business leaders, in Zaleznik's
words "commit themselves to a career in which they have
to work on themselves as a condition for effective working and working with other people."[5] At the same time, a
leader must recognize that "the essence of leadership is
choice, a singularly individualistic act in which a [per-
son] assumes responsibility for a commitment to direct an
organization along a particular path. . . . As much as a
leader wishes to trust others, he has to judge the soundness and validity of his subordinates' positions. Otherwise, the leader may become a prisoner of the emotional
commitments of his subordinates, frequently at the expense of making correct judgments about policies and
strategies."[6]

When a management group is locked in disagreement,
the presence of power and the need for its exercise conditions the dialogue. There are circumstances when the
exercise of leadership must transcend disagreement that
cannot be resolved by discussion. Subordinates, making

---

[5]Abraham Zaleznik and Manfred F. R. Kets de Vries, *Power and the Corporate Mind* (Boston: Houghton Mifflin, 1975), p. 207.
[6]Ibid., p. 209.

the best of the inevitable, must accept a follower role. When leadership becomes irresponsible and dominates subordinate participation without reason, it is usually ineffective or is deposed. Participants in strategic disagreements must not only know their own needs and power but those of the chief executive. Strategic management, in the sense that power attached to value plays a role in it, is a political process.[7]

You should obviously not warp your recommended strategy to the detriment of your company's future in order to adjust it to the personal values you hold or observe. On the other hand, you should not expect to be able to impose without risk and without expectation of eventual vindication and agreement, an unwelcome pattern of purposes and policies on the people in charge of a corporation or responsible for achieving results. Strategy is a human construction; it must in the long run be responsive to human needs. It must ultimately inspire commitment. It must stir an organization to successful striving against competition. Some people have to have their hearts in it.

---

[7]See Abraham Zaleznik: "Managers and Leaders: Are They Different?" *Harvard Business Review*, May–June 1977, pp. 67–78.

Chapter five

The company and its responsibilities to society: Relating corporate strategy to ethical values

We come at last to the fourth component of strategy formulation—the moral and social implications of what once was considered a purely economic choice. In our consideration of strategic alternatives, we have come from what strategists *might* and *can* do to what they *want* to do. We now move to what they *ought* to do—from the viewpoint of various leaders and segments of society and their own standards of right and wrong.

Ethics, like preference, may be considered a product of values. To some the suggestion that an orderly and analytical process of strategy determination should include the discussion of highly controversial ethical issues, about which honest differences of opinion are common and self-deceiving rationalization endless, is repugnant. This body of opinion is led by an immovable and doughty band of economic isolationists, of which Milton Friedman is the leader. They argue that business should be required only to live up to its legal obligations and that consideration of strategic alternatives should be exclusively economic.[1] A larger group of business leaders remain silent, probably suspecting the rhetorical virtue in public statements of corporate intent. A host of small business people are too busy at surviving adversity to dwell much on this subject.

---

[1] The classic statement of this position is still Milton Friedman, *Capitalism and Freedom* (Chicago: The University of Chicago Press, 1962).

THE MORAL COMPONENT OF CORPORATE STRATEGY

The emerging view in the liberal-professional leadership of our most prominent corporations is that determining future strategy must take into account—as part of its social environment—steadily rising moral and ethical standards. Reconciling the conflict in responsibility which occurs when maximum profit and social contribution appear on the same agenda adds to the complexity of strategy formulation and its already clear demands for creativity. Coming to terms with the morality of choice may be the most strenuous undertaking in strategic decision.

Attention is compelled to the noneconomic consequences of corporate power and activity by a combination of forces constituting the environment of business. Most dramatic is the decline in public confidence in public and private institutions accompanying the prosecution of the Vietnam War, Watergate, and the forced resignation of a vice president and president of the United States. Distrust of business flared with the revelation by the Watergate Special Prosecutor of illegal political contributions. The Securities and Exchange Commission's probe of other illegal and questionable payments has publicized the illegal or questionable behavior of scores of well-known companies. The deposition of the top leadership of such companies as the Gulf Oil Corporation and the Lockheed Aircraft Company was a blow to the supposition that our respected companies were abiding by the law and professional standards of ethical conduct. The quick confessions of other companies to avoid prosecution were given wide publicity.

The absence of disavowal by competitors of such practices left the impression with the public that this illegality was characteristic of all business. Successive Harris polls reported that 55 percent of the public in 1966 had felt great confidence in the chief executives of large corporations, that 21 percent felt that way in 1974, and only 15 percent in 1975. A Gallup poll in July 1975 showed big business scored lowest in confidence (34 percent) compared to organized labor (38 percent), Congress (40 percent), the Supreme Court (49 percent), the Executive branch (52 percent), the military (58 percent), education (67 percent), and organized religion (68 percent).[2]

Discussions of the responsibility of business have usually until now taken individual personal integrity for granted or have assumed that the courts were adequate discipline to ensure compliance with the law. The obvious necessity for explicit company policy now makes it necessary for decision to be made about at least how compliance with the law can be ensured. The first step is a stated policy that illegality will not be condoned and enforcement provisions will begin with corporate action rather than waiting for the law and the courts. Thus corporate strategy now must extend beyond the implicit or explicit intention to be law-abiding, to policy designed to cope with the organization problems making obedience to the law difficult to achieve.

Since political contributions and bribery are neither illegal nor even unusual in other parts of the world, explicit policy must be made with respect to other marginal, technically legal, but in American eyes, improper kinds of payments. Once embarked on this path, companies are forced in include policy decisions about other corporate and personal ethical behavior in their

---

[2]Leonard Silk and David Vogel, *Ethics and Profit: The Crisis of Confidence in American Business* (New York: Simon & Schuster, Inc., 1976), pp. 21–22.

strategies. Presumably, except possibly for such policy as proscribing political contributions where they are legally permitted, the economic isolationists would not object to the new necessity to articulate and enforce the unspoken strategic assumption that the company would pursue its economic objectives within the law.

As many a corporation that has regarded itself as socially responsible is finding out, specifying and securing ethical behavior is not easy in a company with responsibility delegated through many levels of authority and degrees of autonomy. The morality of personal behavior, however, is not the only concern. Arguments for active participation in public affairs and the exercise of concern for the impact of economic activity upon society are gaining ground for a number of reasons.

First, corporate executives of the caliber, integrity, intelligence, and humanity capable of coping with the problems of personal morality just cited are not happy to be tarred with the brush of bribery and corruption. They are not likely to turn their backs on other problems involving corporate behavior of the middle and late 70s. The mid-decade recession, the developing energy crisis, the growing sensitivity to environmental damage by industrial and community operations, the protection of the consumer from intended or unwitting exploitation or deception, the extension of social justice, as exemplified by the demands of minority populations and women for opportunity and recognition, the general concern for the limits of growth and the so-called quality of life—all these cannot be ignored. The need is widely acknowledged to respond as a matter of conscience as well as a matter of law.

Second, it is increasingly clear that government regulation is not a good substitute for knowledgeable self-restraint. As expectations for the protection and well-being of the environment, of customers, and of employees grow more insistent, it is clear that if corporate power is to be regulated more by public law than by private conscience, much of our national energy will have to be spent keeping watch over corporate behavior, ferreting out problems, designing and revising detailed laws to deal with them, and enforcing these laws even as they become obsolete.

Executives assuming top management responsibility today may be more sensitive on the average than their predecessors to the upgrading of our goals as a society and more responsive to the opportunity to relate corporate and public purposes. But if not, they can be sure that new regulation will force this concern upon their strategic processes. Extending the reach of strategic decision to encompass public concerns is either a voluntary response permitting latitude in choice or acquiescence to law which may involve none. New forms of regulation or effective enforcement come late to the problem without regard for feasibility or cost. The strategist can consider much earlier whether the problem is susceptible to effective and economically satisfactory solution.

CATEGORIES OF CONCERN

If you elect to admit responsiveness to society's concern about corporate power and activities to your definition of strategy, you come face to face with two major questions. What is the range of corporate involvement available to a company? What considerations should guide its choice of opportunity?

The world.   The problems affecting the quality of life

in the society to which the company belongs may usefully be thought of as extending through a set of densely
populated spheres from the firm itself to the world community. The multinational firm, to take world society
first, would find (within its economic contribution to in-
dustrialization in the developing countries) the need to
measure what it takes out before it could judge its participation responsible. The willingness to undertake joint
ventures rather than insist on full ownership, to share
management and profits in terms not immediately related
to the actual contributions of other partners, to cooperate
otherwise with governments looking for alternatives to
capitalism, to train nationals for skilled jobs and management positions, to reconcile different codes of ethical
practice in matters of taxes and bribery—all illustrate the
opportunity for combining entrepreneurship with responsibility and the terms in which strategy might be expressed.

   The nation.   Within the United States, for a firm of national scope, problems susceptible to constructive attention from business occur in virtually every walk of life. To
narrow too wide a choice, a company would most naturally begin with the environmental consequences of its
manufacturing processes or the impact of its products
upon the public. Presumably a company would first put
its own house in order or embark upon a long program to
make it so. Then it might take interest in other problems,
either through tax-deductible philanthropic contributions or through business ventures seeking economic opportunity in social need—for example, trash disposal or
health care. Education, the arts, race relations, equal opportunity for women, or even such large issues as the impact upon society of technological change compete for attention. Our agenda of national problems is extensive. It

is not hard to find opportunities. The question, as in product-market possibilities, is which ones to choose.

The local community. Closer home are the problems of the communities in which the company operates. These constitute the urban manifestations of the national problems already referred to—inadequate housing, unemployment in the poverty culture, substandard medical care, and the like. The city, special focus of national decay and vulnerable to fiscal and other mismanagement, is an attractive object of social strategy because of its nearness and compactness. The near community allows the development of mutually beneficial corporate projects such as vocational training. Business cannot remain healthy in a sick community.

Industry. Moving from world to country to city takes us through the full range of social and political issues which engage the attention of corporate strategists who wish to factor social responsibility into their planning. Two other less obvious but even more relevant avenues of action should be considered—the industry or industries in which the company operates and the quality of life within the company itself. Every industry, like every profession, has problems which arise from a legacy of indifference, stresses of competition, the real or imagined impossibility of interfirm cooperation under the antitrust laws. Every industry has chronic problems of its own, such as safety, product quality, pricing, and pollution in which only cooperative action can effectively pick up where regulation leaves off or makes further regulation unnecessary.

The company. Within the firm itself, a company has open opportunities for satisfying its aspirations to responsibility. The quality of any company's present strategy, for example, is probably always subject to improvement, as new technology and higher aspirations work together. But besides such important tangible matters as the quality of goods and services being offered to the public and the maintenance and improvement of ordinary craftsmanship, there are three other areas which in the future will become much more important than they seem now. The first of these is the review process set up to estimate the quality of top-management decision. The second is the impact upon individuals of the control systems and other organization processes installed to secure results. The third is a recognition of the role of the individual in the corporation.

Review of management concerns for responsibility

The everyday pressures bearing on decisions about what to do and how to get it done make almost impossible the kind of detached self-criticism which is essential to the perpetuation of responsible freedom. The opportunity to provide for systematic review sessions becomes more explicit and self-conscious. At any rate, as a category of concern, how a management can maintain sufficient detachment to estimate without self-deception the quality of its management performance is as important as any other. The proper role of the board of directors in performing this function—long since lost sight of—requires revitalization.

The caliber and strategic usefulness of a board of directors will nonetheless remain the option of the chief executive who usually determines its function. How much he uses his board for the purposes of improving the quality of corporate strategy and planning turns, as usual, on the sincerity of his interest and his skill. Recent research has illuminated the irresponsibility of inaction in the face of

problems requiring the perspective available only to
properly constituted boards. This organization resource
is available to general managers who recognize dormancy
as waste and seek counsel in cases of conflicting responsibility. A number of large corporations, including
General Motors, have established Public Responsibility
Committees of the board to focus attention on social issues.

The effective provision by a board of responsible surveillance of the moral quality of a management's strategic
decisions means that current stirrings of concern about
conflicts of interest will soon result in the withdrawal
from boards of bankers representing institutions performing services to the company, of lawyers (in some instances) representing a firm retained by the company, and
other suppliers or customers, as well as more scrupulous
attention to present regulations about interlocking interests. As much attention will soon be given to avoiding the
possibility of imputing conflict of interest to a director as
to avoiding the actual occurrence. Stronger restrictions
on conflict of interest will also affect employees of the
firm, including the involvement of individuals with
social-action organizations attacking the firm.

Impact of control systems on ethical performance

Second, the ethical and economic quality of an organization's performance is vitally affected by its control system, which inevitably leads people, if it is effective at all,
to do what will make them look good in the terms of the
system rather than what their opportunities and problems, which the system may not take cognizance of, actually require. We will examine the unintended conse-

quences of control and measurement systems when we come to the implementation of corporate strategy; in the meantime we should note that unanticipated pressures to act irresponsibly may be applied by top management who would deplore this consequence if they knew of it. The process of promotion, by which persons are moved from place to place so fast that they do not develop concern for the problems of the community in which they live or effective relationships within which to accomplish anything, unintentionally weakens the participation of executives in community affairs. The tendency to measure executives in divisionalized companies on this year's profits reduces sharply their motivation to invest in social action with returns over longer times. Lifelong habits of neutrality and noninvolvement eventually deprive the community, in a subtle weakening of its human resources, of executive experience and judgment. Executive cadres are in turn deprived of real-life experience with political and social systems which they ultimately much need.

The individual and the corporation

The actual quality of life in a business organization turns most crucially on how much freedom is accorded to the individual. Certainly most firms consider responsibility to their members a category of concern as important as external constituencies. It is as much a matter of enlightened self-interest as of responsibility to provide conditions encouraging the convergence of the individual's aspirations with those of the corporation, to provide conditions for effective productivity, and to reward employees for extraordinary performance.

With the entry of the corporation into controversial

areas comes greater interest on the part of organization members to take part in public debate. It becomes possible for individuals to make comments on social problems that could be embarrassing to the corporation. It is at best difficult to balance the freedom of individuals and the consequences of their participation in public affairs against the interests of the corporation. The difficulty is increased if the attitudes of management, which are instinctively overprotective of the corporation, are harsh and restrictive. Short-run embarrassments and limited criticism from offended groups—even perhaps a threatened boycott—may be a small price to pay for the continued productivity within the corporation of people whose interests are deep and broad enough to cause them to take stands on public issues. The degree to which an organization is efficient, productive, creative, and capable of development is dependent in large part on the maintenance of a climate in which the individual does not feel suppressed, and in which a kind of freedom (analogous to that which the corporation enjoys in a free enterprise society) is permitted as a matter of course. Overregulation of the individual by corporate policy is no more appropriate internally than overregulation of the corporation by government. On the other hand, personal responsibility is as appropriate to individual liberty as corporate responsibility is to corporate freedom.

The range of concerns

What corporate strategists have to be concerned with, then, ranges from the most global of the problems of world society to the uses of freedom by a single person in the firm. The problems of their country, community, and industry lying between these extremes make opportunity for social contribution exactly coextensive with the range of economic opportunity before them. The problem of choice may be met in the area of responsibility in much the same way as in product-market combinations and in developing a program for growth and diversification.

The business firm, as an organic entity intricately affected by and affecting its environment, is as appropriately adaptive, our concept of corporate strategy suggests, to demands for responsible behavior as for economic service. Special satisfactions and prestige, if not economic rewards, are available for companies that are not merely adaptive but take the lead in shaping the moral and ethical environment within which their primary economic function is performed. Such firms are more persuasive than others, moreover, in convincing the public of the inherent impossibility of satisfying completely all the conflicting claims made upon business.

CHOICE OF STRATEGIC ALTERNATIVES FOR SOCIAL ACTION

The choice of avenues in which to participate will, of course, be influenced by the personal values of the managers making the decision. In the absence of powerful predispositions, the inner coherence of the corporate strategy would be extended by choosing issues most closely related to the economic strategy of the company, to the expansion of its markets, to the health of its immediate environment, and to its own industry and internal problems. The extent of appropriate involvement depends importantly on the resources available. Because the competence of the average corporation outside its economic functions is severely limited, it follows that a company should not venture into good works that are not strategically related to its present and prospective economic functions.

As in the case of personal values and individual idiosyncrasy, a company may be found making decisions erratically related to nonstrategic motives. However noble these may be, they are not made strategic and thus defensible and valid by good intentions alone. Rather than make large contributions to X University because its president is a graduate, it might better develop a pattern of educational support that blends the company's involvement in the whole educational system, its acknowledged debt for the contributions of technical or managerial education to the company, and its other contributions to its communities. What makes participation in public affairs strategic rather than improvisatory is (as we have seen in conceiving economic strategy) a definition of objectives taking all other objectives into account and a plan that reflects the company's definition of itself not only as a purveyor of goods and services but as a responsible institution in its society.

The strategically directed company then will have a strategy for support of community institutions as explicit as its economic strategy and as its decisions about the kind of organization it intends to be and the kind of people it intends to attract to its membership. It is easy and proper, when margins allow it, to make full use of tax deductibility, through contributions, from which it expects no direct return. The choice of worthy causes, however, should relate to the company's concept of itself and thus directly to its economic mission. It should enter into new social service fields with the same questions about its resources and competence that new product-market combinations inspire. In good works as in new markets, opportunity without the competence to develop it is illusory. Deliberate concentration on limited objectives is preferable to scattered short-lived enthusiasm across a community's total need.

Policy for ethical and moral personal behavior, once the level of integrity has been decided, is not complicated by a wide range of choice. The nature of the company's operations defines the areas of vulnerability—purchasing, rebates, price-fixing, fee-splitting, customs facilitation, bribery, dubious agents' fees, conflict of interest, theft, or falsification of records. Where problems appear or danger is sensed specific rules can be issued. As in the case of government regulation of the firm, these should not be overdetailed or mechanical, for there is no hope of anticipating the ingenuity of the willful evader. Uncompromising penalties for violations of policy intent or the rarely specified rule will do more to clarify strategy in this area than thousands of words beforehand. The complexity of elevating individual behavior is thus a matter of implementation of strategy more properly discussed in the context of organization processes such as motivation and control.

DETERMINATION OF STRATEGY

We have now before us the major determinants of strategy. The principal aspects of formulation are (1) appraisal of present and foreseeable opportunity and risk in the company's environment, (2) assessment of the firm's unique combination of present and potential corporate resources or competences, (3) determination of the noneconomic personal and organizational preferences to be satisfied, and (4) identification and acceptance of the social responsibilities of the firm. The strategic decision is one that can be reached only after all these factors have been considered and the action implications of each assessed.

In your efforts to analyze the situation of your own organization, you have experienced much more of the problem of the strategist than can be described on paper. When you have relinquished your original idea as to what a company's strategy should be in favor of a more imaginative one, you have seen that the formulation process has an essential creative and entrepreneurial aspect. In your effort to differentiate your thinking about your company from the conventional thinking of its industry, you may have become alert to new opportunities and new applications of corporate competence. You may still find it strange to define a product in terms of its present and potential functions rather than of its physical properties. You have probably made a start on how to assess the special competence of your firm from its past accomplishments, and how to identify values and aspirations. You may have tried to rank preferences in order of their strength—your own among others.

The problem implicit in striking a balance between the company's apparent opportunity and its evident competence, between your own personal values and concepts of responsibility and those of the company's other members, is not an easy one. The concepts we have been discussing should help you make a decision, but they will not determine your decision for you. Whenever choice is compounded of rational analysis which can have more than one outcome, of aspiration and desire which can run the whole range of human ambition, and a sense of responsibility which changes the appeal of alternatives, it cannot

be reduced to quantitative approaches or to the exactness
which management science can apply to narrower questions. Managers contemplating strategic decisions must be
willing to make them without the guidance of decision
rules, with confidence in their own judgment, which will
have been seasoned by repeated analyses of similar questions. They must be aware that more than one decision is
possible and that they are not seeking the single right answer. They can take encouragement from the fact that the
manner in which an organization implements the chosen
program can help to validate the original decision.

Some of the most difficult choices confronting a company are those which must be made among several alternatives that appear equally attractive and also equally desirable. Once the analysis of opportunity has produced an
inconveniently large number of possibilities, any firm has
difficulty in deciding what it wants to do and how the
new activities will be related to the old.

In situations where opportunity is approximately equal
and economic promise is offered by a wide range of activities, the problem of making a choice can be reduced
by reference to the essential character of the company and
to the kind of company the executives wish to run. The
study of alternatives from this point of view will sooner
or later reveal the greater attractiveness of some choices
over others. Economic analysis and calculations of return
on investment, though of course essential, may not crucially determine the outcome. Rather, the logjam of decision can only be broken by a frank exploration of executive aspirations regarding future development, including
perhaps the president's own wishes with respect to the
kind of institution he or she prefers to head, carried on as
part of a free and untrammeled investigation of what
human needs the organization would find satisfaction in

serving. That return on investment alone will point the way ignores the values implicit in the calculations and the contribution which an enthusiastic commitment to new projects can make. The rational examination of alternatives and the determination of purpose are among the most important and most neglected of all human activities. The final decision, which should be made as deliberately as possible after a detailed consideration of the issues we have attempted to separate, is an act of will and desire as much as of intellect.

Chapter six

The accomplishment
of purpose:
Strategy and organization

We now turn our attention to the concepts and skill essential to the implementation of strategy. The life of action requires more than analytical intelligence. It is not enough to have an idea and be able to evaluate its worth. Persons with responsibility for the achievement of goals, the accomplishment of results, and the solution of problems, finally know the worth of a strategy when its power is demonstrated. Furthermore, a unique corporate strategy determined in relation to a concrete situation is never complete, even as a formulation, until it is embodied in the organizational activities which reveal its soundness and begin to affect its nature. Even then it will continue to evolve.

INTERDEPENDENCE OF FORMULATION AND IMPLEMENTATION

It is convenient from the point of view of orderly study to divide a consideration of corporate strategy, as we have done, into aspects of formulation and implementation and to note, for example, the requirement of the former for analytical and conceptual ability and of the latter for administrative skill. But in real life the processes of formulation and implementation are intertwined. Feedback from operations gives notice of changing environmental factors to which strategy should be adjusted. The formulation of strategy is not finished when implementation begins. A business organization is always changing in response to its own makeup and past development. Similarly, it should be changing in response to changes in the larger systems in which it moves, and in response to its success or failure in affecting its environment. For the sake of orderly presentation, we now focus less on what the strategy should be than on ways to make it effective in action and to alter it as required.

We have already seen that the determination of strategy has four continuous subactivities: the examination of the environment for opportunity and risk, the systematic assessment of corporate strengths and weaknesses, the identification and weighting of personal values, and the clarification of social responsibility. Implementation may also be thought of as having important subactivities. In very broad terms, these are the design of organizational structure and relationships for the execution and adaptation of strategy, and the effective administration of organizational processes affecting behavior. Finally the management of the strategic process itself, which we shall call strategic management for short, may be viewed as the essence of corporate governance. We come then to the strategic function of the board of directors. This body itself requires leadership, usually but not always by the chief executive, who presides over the formulation and implementation activities at other levels of the organization.

In deciding or confirming strategy, senior executives (in our practitioner's theory) range over the whole vast territory of the technological, social, economic, ecological, and political systems which provide opportunity for their company or threaten its continued existence. When they turn their attention to carrying out the strategy tentatively determined, they are apparently required to address themselves, within the limitations of their knowledge, to all the techniques and skills of administration.

To deal with so wide a range of activity, they need a simple and flexible approach to the aspects of organized activity which they must take into account. By considering the relationships between strategy and organizational structure, strategy and organizational processes, and reconceiving strategy itself as an organization process that can be managed, the reader should be able to span a territory crowded with ideas without losing sight of the purpose sought in crossing it.

Each of the implementing subactivities constitutes in itself a special world in which many people are doing research, developing knowledge, and asserting the importance of their work over that of other specialists. Thus the nature of organization, about which every general manager must make some assumptions, is the subject of a richly entangled array of ideas upon which one could spend a lifetime. The design of information systems—particularly at a time when the speed and capacity of the computer continue to fascinate the processors of information—appears to require long study, an esoteric language, and even rearrangement of organizational activities for the sake of information processing. Similarly, performance appraisal, motivation and incentive systems, control systems, and systems of executive recruitment, development, and compensation all have their armies of theoretical and empirical proponents, each one fully equipped with manuals, code books, rules, and techniques.

It will, of course, be impossible for us to consider here in detail the knowledge and theory which have been developed during the course of a half century of researches in administration. It will be assumed that your own experience has introduced you to the major schools of thought contending in the developing administrative disciplines. Just as general managers must be able to draw upon the skills of special staffs in leading their organizations, so they must be able to draw upon these special studies in effecting their own combination of organizational design and organizational practices. The simple prescription we wish to add here is that *the corporate strategy must dominate the design of organizational structure and processes.* That is, the principal criterion for all decisions on organizational structure and behavior should be their relevance to the achievement of organizational purpose, not their conformity to the dictates of special disciplines. A clear perception of strategy enables one to sort out and discard most of the prescriptions generated by a theoretical and abstract consideration of organization. It follows that seeking out a coherent strategic pattern of purpose and policy is more important than mastery of organization principles and theory.

Thus the theses we suggest for your consideration are first that conscious strategy can be consciously implemented through skills primarily administrative in nature. Second, the chief determinant of organizational structure and the processes by which tasks are assigned and performance motivated, rewarded, and controlled should be *the strategy of the firm*, not the history of the company, its position in its industry, the specialized background of its executives, the principles of organization as developed in textbooks, the recommendations of consultants, or the conviction that one form of organization is intrinsically better than another.

The successful implementation of strategy requires that executives shape to the peculiar needs of their strategy the formal structure of their organization, its informal relationships, and the processes of motivation and control which provide incentives and measure results.

They try to bring about the commitment to organizational aims and policies of properly qualified individuals and groups to whom portions of the total task have been assigned. They must ensure not only that goals are clear and purposes are understood, but also that individuals are developing in terms of compensation and personal satisfactions. Above all, they must do what they can to arrange that departmental interests, interdepartmental rivalries, and the machinery of measurement and evaluation do not deflect energy from organizational purpose into harmful or irrelevant activity.

To clarify our approach to the problem of adapting the concepts and findings of special disciplines to the requirements of policy, we summarize here some aspects of implementation that may serve as a convenient map of the territory to be traversed. This list is designed only to make it possible for you to use your own specialized knowledge and adapt it, within limits imposed by your own characteristic attitudes toward risk and responsibility, to strategic requirements.

1.   Once strategy is tentatively or finally set, the key tasks to be performed and kinds of decisions required must be identified.

2.   Once the size of operations exceeds the capacity of one person, responsibility for accomplishing key tasks and making decisions must be assigned to individuals or groups. The division of labor must permit efficient performance of subtasks and must be accomplished by some hierarchical allocation of authority to assure achievement.

3.   Formal provisions for the coordination of activities thus separated must be made in various ways, e.g., through a hierarchy of supervision, project and commit-

tee organizations, task forces, and other *ad hoc* units. The prescribed activities of these formally constituted bodies are not intended to preclude spontaneous voluntary coordination.

4. Information systems adequate for coordinating divided functions (i.e., for letting those performing part of the task know what they must know of the rest, and for letting those in supervisory positions know what is happening so that next steps may be taken) must be designed and installed.

5. The tasks to be performed should be arranged in a sequence comprising a program of action or a schedule of targets to be achieved at specified times. While long-range plans may be couched in relatively general terms, operating plans will often take the form of relatively detailed budgets. These can meet the need for the establishment of standards against which short-term performance can be judged.

6. Actual performance, as quantitatively reported in information systems and qualitatively estimated through observation by supervisors and judgment of customers, should be compared to budgeted performance and to standards in order to test achievement, budgeting processes, the adequacy of the standards, and the competence of individuals.

7. Individuals and groups of individuals must be recruited and assigned to essential tasks in accordance with the specialized or supervisory skills which they possess or can develop. At the same time, the assignment of tasks may well be adjusted to the nature of available skills.

8. Individual performance, evaluated both quantitatively and qualitatively, should be subjected to influences (constituting a pattern of incentives) which will help to make it effective in accomplishing organizational goals.

9. Since individual motives are complex and multi-

ple, incentives for achievement should range from those
that are universally appealing—such as adequate compensation and an organizational climate favorable to the
simultaneous satisfaction of individual and organizational purposes—to specialized forms of recognition, financial or nonfinancial, designed to fit individual needs
and unusual accomplishments.

10.   In addition to financial and nonfinancial incentives and rewards to motivate individuals to voluntary
achievement, a system of constraints, controls, and penalties must be devised to contain nonfunctional activity
and to enforce standards. Controls, like incentives, are
both formal and informal. Effective control requires both
quantitative and nonquantitative information, which
must always be used together.

11.   Provision for the continuing development of requisite technical and managerial skills is a high-priority
requirement. The development of individuals must take
place chiefly within the milieu of their assigned responsibilities. This on-the-job development should be
supplemented by intermittent formal instruction and
study.

12.   Energetic personal leadership is necessary for
continued growth and improved achievement in any organization. Leadership may be expressed in many styles,
but it must be expressed in some perceptible style. This
style must be natural and also consistent with the requirements imposed upon the organization by its strategy
and membership.

The general manager is principally concerned with determining and monitoring the adequacy of strategy, with
adapting the firm to changes in its environment, and with
securing and developing the people needed to carry out

the strategy or to help with its constructive revision or evolution. Managers must also ensure that the processes which encourage and constrain individual performance and personal development are consistent with human and strategic needs. In large part, therefore, leadership consists of achieving commitments to strategy via clarification and dramatization of its requirements and value.

We shall return to each of these considerations, looking first at some general relationships between strategy and organizational structure. We shall look also at the need for specialization of tasks, coordination of divided responsibility, and the design of effective information systems.

STRATEGY AND ORGANIZATIONAL STRUCTURE

It is at once apparent that the accomplishment of strategic purpose requires organization. If a consciously formulated or coherently evolutionary strategy is to be effective, organizational development should be planned rather than left to evolve by itself. So long as a company is small enough for a single individual to direct both planning for the future and current operations, questions of organizational structure remain unimportant. Thus the one-man organization encounters no real organizational problem until the proprietor's quick walks through the plant, his wife's bookkeeping, and his sales agent's marketing activities are no longer adequate to growing volume. When the magnitude of operations increases, then departmentalization—usually into such clusters of activities as manufacturing, production, and finance—begins to appear. Most functional organizations ultimately encounter size problems again. With geographical dispersion, product complexity, and increased volume of sales, coordination must be accomplished somewhere else than at the top. We then find multiunit organizations with coordinating responsibility delegated to divisions, subsidiaries, profit centers, and the like. The difficulty of designing an organizational structure is directly proportionate to the diversity and size of the undertaking and to the clarity of its strategy.

The subject of organization is the most extensive and complex of all the subtopics of implementation. It has at various times attracted the interest of economists, sociologists, psychologists, political scientists, philosophers, and, in a curiously restricted way, of creative writers as well. These have contributed to the field a variety of theoretical formulations and empirical investigations. The policy maker will probably find himself unable to subscribe wholeheartedly to the precepts of any one school of thought or to the particulars of any one model of the firm. Indeed, established theories of the firm are inadequate for general management purposes. The impact of most organizational studies, from the point of view of the eclectic practitioner looking for counsel rather than confusion, has been to undermine confidence in other studies. The activities of present-day social science have in particular badly damaged the precepts of classical scientific management.

Regardless of disputes about theory among scholars, the executive in, say, a company that has reached some complexity, knows three things: The tasks essential to accomplishing purpose must in some way be subdivided; they must be assigned, if possible, to individuals whose skills are appropriately specialized; and tasks that have been subdivided must ultimately be reintegrated into a unified whole. The manager knows also that once performance is out of one pair of hands, and once no one in the organization is performing the total task, information about what one group is doing must be made available to the others. Otherwise problems and risks cannot be detected and dealt with.

SUBDIVISION OF TASK RESPONSIBILITY

In every industry conventional ways of dividing task by function have developed to the extent that the training of individuals skilled in these functions perpetuates organizational arrangements. But identification of the tasks *should* be made in terms of a company's distinctive purposes and unique strategy, not by following industry convention. True, the fact that every manufacturing firm procures and processes raw materials and sells and delivers finished products means that at least production and sales and probably procurement and distribution will always be critical functional areas which must be assigned to specialized organizational units. But these basic uniformities which cut across company and industry lines provide the individual firm with little useful guidance on the issues it finds so perplexing—namely, how much weight to assign to which function, or how to adapt nearly universal structural arrangements to its own particular needs.

A manufacturer who plans to perform services for the government under cost-plus-fixed-fee contracts, to cite a very limited example, feels less need for a fully developed cost control system and cost-related incentives than one whose contracts are governed by a fixed price. To illustrate more broadly the way in which strategic choice determines the relative importance of tasks, consider the manufacturer of a line of industrial products who decides to diversify in view of declining opportunity in the original field. Product improvement and the engineering organization responsible for it become less vital than the search for new products, either internally or through acquisition. But if the latter task is not recognized as crucial, then it is unlikely to be assigned to any individual or unit, but will rather be considered an additional duty for many. Under the latter circumstances, little will get done.

Once the key tasks have been identified (or the identification customary in the industry has been ratified as proper for the individual firm), then responsibility for accomplishing these tasks must be assigned to individuals and groups. In addition to a rational principle for separating tasks from one another, the need will soon become apparent for some scale of relative importance among activities to be established.

Distribution of formal authority among those to whom tasks have been assigned is essential for the effective control of operations, the development of individual skills, the distribution of rewards, and for other organizational processes to which we shall soon give attention. The extent to which individuals, once assigned a task, need to be supervised and controlled is the subject of voluminous argument which, temporarily at least, must leave the general practitioner aware that too much control and too little are equally ineffective and that, as usual, the generalist is the person who must strike the balance.

The division of labor is thus accompanied by the specialization of task and the distribution of authority, with the relative importance of tasks as defined by strategy marked by status. The rational principle by which tasks are specialized and authority delegated may be separation by functions, by product or product lines, by geographical or regional subdivision, by customer and market, or by type of production equipment or processes. The intermixture of these principles in multiunit organizations has resulted in many hybrid types of formal structure which we need not investigate.

The principal requirement is that the basis for division should be relatively consistent, easily understood, and conducive to the grouping of like activities. Above all, the formal pattern should have visible relationship to corporate purpose, should fix responsibility in such a way as not to preclude teamwork, and should provide for the solution of problems as close to the point of action as possible. In an organization governed by purpose, responsibility will often exceed authority (contrary to the classical doctrine of absolute equality); the resulting ambiguity provides opportunity for initiative and clarification in terms of shared objectives rather than separate fiefdoms. Structure should not be any more restrictive than necessary of the satisfaction of individual needs or of the inevitable emergence of informal organization. The design should also allow for more complex structure as the organization grows in size.

As you consider the need to create, build, and develop an organizational structure, you will wish to avoid choosing a pattern of organization on the grounds that it is "typical" or "generally sound." Any preference you may have for divisional versus functional organizations, for decentralized rather than centralized decision making, for a "flat" rather than a "steep" or many-stepped hierarchy, should be set aside until you have identified the activities made essential by the strategy, the skills available for their performance, and the needs and values of the individuals involved. The plan you devise should ignore

neither the history of the company nor that of its industry,
for in ongoing organizations formal structure may not be
abruptly changed without great cost. Any new plan that
you devise for gradual implementation should be as
economical as is consistent with the requirements for
technical skill, proper support for principal functions,
and reserve capacity for further growth. The degree of
centralization and decentralization that you prescribe
should not turn on your personal preference, and certainly will vary from one activity to another. Strategic
requirements as well as the abilities and experience of
company executives should determine the extent to
which responsibility for decisions should tend toward
the center or toward the field. In a consumer credit company, for example, freedom to extend credit to doubtful
risks can really be allowed only to relatively experienced
branch managers although company strategy may prescribe it for all.

That so little need be said about the nature of the formal organization, and so much must be determined by
the particulars of each individual situation, should not be
taken as evidence that formal organization does not matter. On the contrary, progress in a growing organization is
impossible without substrategies for organizational development. Restructuring the organization becomes a
subgoal to be worked toward over a period of years—
perhaps without the interim publication of the ultimate
design.

But though it is impractical, except in cases of harsh
emergency, to make sweeping organizational changes
with little preparation and upon short notice, this is not
to say that no major role is played by structure, by clear
and logical subdivisions of task, or by an openly
acknowledged hierarchy of authority, status, and pres-

tige—all serving as the conscious embodiment of strategy and the harbinger of growth to come. As you check the relation between strategy and structure, whether in your study of cases or in your business experience, ask yourself always the policy questions: Is the strategy sound and clear? If goals are clear, have the tasks required been clearly identified and assessed for their relative importance? If key activities are known, have they been assigned to people with the requisite training, experience, and staff support? If not are such people being sought? The answers to these questions do not carry one very far along the road toward successful strategy implementation, but they provide a convenient starting point.

COORDINATION OF DIVIDED RESPONSIBILITY

As soon as a task is divided, some formal provision must be made for coordination. In baseball, the park outside the diamond is subdivided into left, center, and right fields, and a player is assigned to each. But if there is no procedure for handling a ball hit halfway between any two areas, the formal division of labor will help only the team at bat and put colliding players on the injured list. Most important work in organizations requires cooperation among the departmental specialists to whom a portion of the total task has been allocated. Many forces are at work to make coordination so essential that it cannot be left to chance. For example, the flow of work from one station to another and from one administrative jurisdiction to another creates problems of scheduling and timing, of accommodating departmental needs, and of overall supervision lest departmental needs become more influential than organizational goals.

As soon as additional people join the first person in an organization, they bring with them their own goals, and these must be served, at least to a minimal degree, by the activity required of them in service to the organization. As soon as a group of such individuals, different in personal needs but similar in technical competence and point of view, is established to perform a given function, then departmental goals may attract more loyalty than the overall goals of the organization. To keep individual purposes and needs as well as departmental substrategies consistent with corporate strategy is, as we have said before, a considerable undertaking. It is a major top-management responsibility in all organizations, regardless of the degree of commitment and willingness to cooperate in the common cause.

The different needs of individuals and the distinctive goals of functional specialties mean that, at best, the organization's total strategy is understood differently and valued for different reasons by different parts of the organization. Some formal or informal means for resolving these differences is important. Where the climate is right, specialists will be aware of the relative validity of organizational and departmental needs and of the bias inevitable in any loyalty to expertise.

Formal organization provides for the coordination of divided responsibility through the hierarchy of supervision, through the establishment and use of committees, and through the project form of organization (which, like temporary task forces, can be superimposed upon a functional or divisional organization). The wider the sphere of any supervisor's jurisdiction, the more time is needed to bring into balance aspects of organized life which would otherwise influence performance toward the wrong goals. The true function of a committee—and were this role more widely understood and effectively played, committees would be less frequently maligned—is to bring to the exploration and solution of interdepartmental problems both the specialist and generalist abilities of its members. The need for formal committees would be largely obviated in an ideal organization, where all members were conscious of the impact of their own proposals, plans, and decisions upon the interests of others. To the extent that individual managers seek out advice and approval from those whose interests must be balanced with theirs, they perform in face-to-face encounters the essential coordination which is sometimes formalized in a committee structure.

Coordination can play a more creative role than merely composing differences. It is the quality of the way in which subdivided functions and interests are resynthesized that often distinguishes one organization from another in terms of results. The reintegration of the parts into the whole, when what is at stake is the execution of corporate strategy, creates a whole that is greater than the sum of its parts. Rivalry between competing subunits or individuals—if monitored to keep it *constructive* rivalry—can exhibit creative characteristics. It can be the source of a new solution to a problem, one that transcends earlier proposals that reflected only the rival units' parochial concerns. The ability to handle the coordinating function in a way that brings about a new synthesis among competing interests, a synthesis in harmony with the special competence of the total organization, is the administrator's most subtle and creative contribution to the successful functioning of an organization.

EFFECTIVE DESIGN OF INFORMATION SYSTEMS

If corporate strategy is to be effectively implemented,

there must be organizational arrangements to provide members with the information they will need to perform their tasks and relate their work to that of others. Information flows inward from the environment to all organizational levels; within the company it should move both down and up. In view of the bulk of information moving upward, it must be reduced to manageable compass as it nears the top. This condensation can be accomplished only by having data synthesized at lower levels, so that part of what moves upward is interpretation rather than fact. To achieve synthesis without introducing distortion or bias or serious omission is a formidable problem to which management must remain alert. Well handled, the information system brings to the attention of those who have authority to act not the vast mass of routine data processed by the total system, but the significant red-flag items that warn of outcomes contrary to expectations. A well-designed information system is thus the key to "management by exception." This in turn is one key to the prevailing problem of the overburdened executive.

In the gathering and transmitting of information, accounting and control departments play a major task. One obstacle to effective performance here is devotion to specialty and procedure for its own sake, as accountants look more to their forms than to larger purposes. The Internal Revenue Service, the Securities and Exchange Commission, the Census Bureau, The Environmental Protection Agency, and the Justice Department, all with requirements which must be met, impose uniformities on the ways in which information is collected and analyzed. But nothing in the conventions of accounting, the regulations of the government, or the rapidly advancing mathematical approaches to problem solving in any way prevents the generation and distribution within an organization of the kind of information management finds must useful.

Now, with the speed of the computer, data can be made available early enough to do some good. We shall have much more to say about the uses of information when we turn to the organizational processes that determine individual behavior. It is important to note that the generation of data is not an end in itself. Its function should be to permit individuals who necessarily perform only one of the many tasks required by the organizational mission to know what they need to know in order to perform their functions in balance with all others, and to gain that overview of total operations which will inform and guide the decisions they have discretion to make. To be useful it must be kept simple. Designing the flow of information is just as important as choosing a principle of subdivision in outlining organizational structure. Information is often the starting point in trying to determine how the organi zation should be changed. It is a way to monitor the con tinuing adequacy of strategy and to warn when change is necessary.

STRATEGY AS THE KEY TO SIMPLICITY

Strategy is conceived and implemented only in combinations of people to some degree "organized" or deployed in compatible task assignments. The strategy for each organization—in our conception of strategic management—will be in some ways unique, because of distinctiveness of competence and pervasion of values. The uniqueness of a company's strategy, in turn, is the key element in organization design. It is strategy, we have said, that should determine structure and the nature of the processes going on throughout the structure. This essential element of our conception puts an early end to our generalizations about how to organize. Until we know the strategy we cannot begin to specify the appropriate structure. This exposition cannot advise you whether a functional or divisional organization is appropriate to the strategy you will be working as a manager to implement, although it is clear that in growing and diversifying organizations the functional form will ordinarily precede the divisional and follow along after as divisions are functionalized. Matrix management you can take or leave alone until you get to the situation itself; all you need to know now is that the key competing considerations— geographical specialization versus worldwide product management, for example—must somehow be integrated in a working equilibrium with strategic importance specifying the weights in the balance.

The elements of thinking like a general manager that we have recommended to you are inert until they are applied to the managerial circumstances in which you find yourself. The assignment of primacy to the application of an idea rather than to its elegant theoretical development is anathema to orthodox theorists. It is inconvenient for those persons expecting to be equipped with the latest and best tools for the solution of management problems and a jargon with which to demonstrate their sophistication. But that the concept of strategy comes to full development only in the unique combination of circumstances in which any organization exists is a simplifying property of the idea that provides it much of its power in action.

If you acquire the ability to think strategically, you will be able to lay aside the burdens of management conceived of as a science which your education has laid upon you and tried to require you to remember. The more highly developed theories and propositions of most of the management sciences are either largely inapplicable or inappropriately applied, for they are usually presented by dedicated partisans as universally applicable. As a phenomenon of management the uniqueness of situations properly takes primacy over the substance of the management disciplines. As we are unable to tell you in detail how to design an organization until we know the purposes you are organizing for and the resources available, we can say there is no one best way to organize. At the same time the quest for purpose prevents organization aimlessness or drifting.

A related paradox presents itself as we consider the unlikelihood that the strategy we have said should always govern will be clear and complete at any one time. Since purpose evolves ordinarily over time as the components of strategy (environmental change and internal resources, for example) develop, it can dictate no final answer in terms of organization structure and process even in the situational context. The structure and processes in place will in fact affect the strategy. If you have profit centers, divisions, or subsidiaries charged with medium and long-term success, they are likely to develop strategically significant innovations simply because divisionalization produces commitment to divison rather than to parent organization. If you send fur buyers to Alaska instructed under quotas only to buy skins, they may end up selling groceries and other necessities to the trappers and incrementally make your fur business into a worldwide trading company. Strategy follows structure in real life, just as it sometimes precedes it there.

What is important now is that in part structure is

strategy. If, in short, the process of strategy formulation, as it must be, is distributed throughout an organization, the shape of that organization and the influences that motivate it will be reflected in the strategy it produces. The strategic decision must, of course, be made in the light of organization and human consequences. Furthermore, it must be arrived at recognizing the constraint of structure and systems derived from previous strategy which influence the generation of new alternatives. Context is both supportive and inhibiting. It may be necessary to change organization before certain strategic alternatives can be fully explored or experimentally attempted.

The subunits of an organization established to implement a given corporate purpose soon will develop divergent strategies to support their own growth and development, especially if responsibility for profit and growth has been assigned to those units. It is true, therefore, that the organization processes and measurement systems by which the functioning of the structure is evaluated will influence strategy. When an international company once tried to interest its Latin-American subsidiaries in profit rather than in the number of sewing machines sold, the country managers, inexperienced but responsive, began making ice cream, selling insurance, and manufacturing stove grates in unused plant space. These diversifications, all aimed at increasing profitability within one year, changed, at least for a time, the local strategy of this company. The structure—geographically discrete and relatively autonomous profit centers—and the incentive system—reward for short-run profitability—together could ultimately have changed the strategy of the entire company. As it happens it was the corporate intention that the company go through a transition emphasizing profitability while its future strategy, too difficult a question for anybody in a company unused to strategic planning to settle, became a problem which could be managed.

Worldwide, the result of similar experiments was a company that faltered between being an appliance and electronics firm or an industrial and consumer products company without the resources or the organization form to make so wide a diversification work. The neglect of the sewing machine business, suffering under Japanese competition, and years of resulting losses led at long last to the dismissal of the responsible executive. He had known his company needed to be profit conscious, but he could not institutionalize a way to deal continuously with the decision of what businesses to be in. His effective stimuli sent the strategic process into a gallop in all directions.

The present management, incidentally, has written off most of the extraneous activities and appears to be concentrating on the historic capability that made the company the first great American multinational corporation. In this instance strategy was made chaotic by change in organization structure and compensation systems. The country managers were neither provided with nor required to develop a new strategy for their areas. A communicable corporate strategy was not generated at company headquarters to give coherent guidance to local initiatives.

Strategic management in the real world then contends with the alternatives generated by organization form and the administrative processes affecting the motivation of people. While the uncertainties of decision about new alternatives delay clear-cut major changes in direction, hundreds of minor decisions incrementally may change the nature of the business and affect the character of the organization.

The real-life development of strategy must be superimposed upon the natural tendency of persons to "satisfice" (if you have read Herbert Simon) or (if you have not) to settle on the first satisfactory, rather than the best, solution to a problem. It envelops and influences the direction of the incrementalism by which organizations devise *ad hoc* responses to new occurrences. It extends the bounds of rationality within which persons and groups react to challenge from the market and social environment. It disciplines the bargaining that can characterize the behavior of coalitions in organizations politicized by strategic uncertainty or dissatisfaction with the objectives and supporting policies in place.

The conclusion that attention to the conscious and deliberate choice of purpose can affect all aspects of an organization is in a sense a reassertion of the role in complex organizations of purposeful rationality. Strategy will evolve over time, no matter what. It will be affected by the consequences of its implementation. But the elucidation of goals can transcend incrementalism to make it a series of forays and experiments evaluated continuously against stated goals to result in the deliberate amendment of strategy or in the curtailment of strategic erosion. All organizations must be focused in purpose in order to avoid outstripping their resources or squandering their distinctive advantage.

The literature of organization theory is by itself, as we have said, of very little use in managing a live organization. What managers gain in discovering this fact is not that there is an advantage to being ignorant but that a powerful unitary idea can be developed in detail in a business situation which they and their associates can know better than anybody else. Selection from what is available to educated generalists and known by specialists concentrating in techniques applicable to classes of narrow problems becomes effective when the relation of specialized knowledge to key problems of organization is recognized as stategically relevant. Knowledge of the evolving situation is more important and practicable than mastering the whole corpus of management booklearning. A rational procedure for comprehending the strategic posture of an organization, for seeing the intuitive purpose in its incremental development, and for assessing the extent to which its structure is effective in the performance of key tasks is much easier come by. It requires experience, judgment, and skill, rather than general knowledge as such, for strategic management is and will remain more an art than a science. Artistic accomplishment depends heavily on the education, sensitivity, competence, and point of view of the artist. Simplicity is the essence of good art; a conception of strategy brings simplicity to complex organizations.

Chapter seven

The accomplishment
of purpose:
Organizational processes
and behavior

Our study of strategy has brought us to the prescription that organizational structure must follow strategy if implementation is to be effective. We have seen that structural design involves inevitably (1) a suitable specialization of task, (2) a parallel provision for coordination, and (3) information systems for meeting the requirement that specialists be well informed and their work coordinated and that general managers know that operations are proceeding as planned. We have seen that a variety of structures may be suitable to a strategy so long as the performance influenced by structural characteristics is not diverted from strategic ends.

We turn now from structural considerations to other influences upon organizational behavior. A logical structure does not ensure effective organized effort any more than a high degree of technical skill in individual members ensures achievement of organizational purposes. We suggest the following proposition for the test of experience: Organizational performance is effective to the extent that individual energy is successfully directed toward organizational goals in an atmosphere deliberately created to encourage the development of required skills and to provide the satisfactions of personal progress. Convergence of energy upon purpose is made effective by individual and group commitment to purpose.

Man-made and natural organizational *systems* and *processes* are available to influence individual development and performance. In any organization the system which relates specific influences upon behavior to each other (so as to constitute an ultimate impact upon behavior) is made up of some six elements: (1) standards, (2) measures, (3) incentives, (4) rewards, (5) penalties, and (6) controls. The distinguishing characteristic of a system, of course, is the interaction of its elements. The interdependence will vary from organization to organization and from situation to situation and cannot always be observed, controlled, or completely analyzed. Despite the systems that serve it, adminstration remains an art.

The familiar processes that bear on performance are (1) measurement, (2) evaluation, (3) motivation, (4) control, and (5) individual development. The most important motor aspects of a process are the speed and direction of its forward motion and the nature of its side effects. So far as the uniqueness of each company situation allows, we shall look at combinations of these organizational systems and processes in the following order:

1. The establishment of standards and measurement of performance.
2. The administration of motivation and incentive systems.
3. The operation of systems of restraint and control.
4. The recruitment and development of management.

These processes have been studied in detail by specialists of several kinds. We shall not attempt to extract all the wisdom or expose all the folly which, over the years, has accumulated in the study of human relations and organizational behavior. We are now concerned, as always, with the limited but important ways in which specialized bodies of knowledge can be put to use in the implementation of strategy. The idea of strategy will dominate our approach to the internal organizational systems which animate structure, just as it dominated our discussion of the factors that determine structure itself. It may be useful to point out that our aim is not to coerce and manipulate unwilling individuals. It is instead to support and direct individuals who are at least assenting to or, more desirably, are commited to organizational goals. Commitment to purpose remains in our scheme of things the overriding necessary condition of effective accomplishment.

ESTABLISHMENT OF STANDARDS AND MEASUREMENT OF PERFORMANCE

If progress toward goals is to be supervised at all, it will have to be observed and measured. If it is to be measured, whether quantitatively or qualitatively, there must be some idea of where an organization is compared to where it ought to be. To state where an organization ought to be is to set a standard. A standard takes shape as a projection of hoped-for or budgeted performance. As time passes, positive and negative variances between budgeted and actual performance are recorded. This comparison makes possible, although it does not necessarily justify, relating incentives and controls to performance as measured against standards. For example, managers in the Hilton Hotels group prepare detailed forecasts of their anticipated revenues, costs, and operating profits, all based on past records and future projections that take growth targets into account. The reward system recognizes not only good results but accuracy of forecasting.

It is virtually impossible to make meaningful generalizations about how proper standards might be set in particular companies. It can be said, however, that in any organization the overall strategy can be translated into more or less detailed future plans (the detail becoming less predictable as the time span grows longer), which permit comparison of actual with predicted performance. Whether standards are being set at exactly the proper level is less significant than the fact that an effort is being made to raise them steadily as organizational power and resources increase. External events may, however, invalidate predictions. It must be recognized that, for good reasons as well as bad, standards are not always attainable. Hence the need for skill in variable budgeting.

By far the most important problem of measurement is that increased interest in the measurement of performance against standards brings increased danger that the executive evaluation program may encourage performance which detracts from rather than supports the overall strategy.

The temptation to use measurement primarily for the purpose of judging executive performance is acute. The desire to put management responsibility in the ablest hands leads to comparing managers in terms of results. Failure to meet a standard leads naturally to the assignment of blame to persons. The general manager's most urgent duty is to see that planned results are indeed accomplished. Such pressure, unfortunately, may lead to exaggerated respect for specific measures and for the short-run results they quantify, and thus to ultimate misevaluation of performance.

Fallacy of the single criterion

The problems of measurement cluster about the fallacy of the single criterion. When any single measure like return on investment, for example, is used to determine the compensation, promotion, or reassignment of a manager, the resultant behavior will often lead to unplanned and undesired outcomes. No single measure can encompass the total contribution of an individual either to immediate and longer term results or to the efforts of others. The sensitivity of individuals to evaluation leads them to produce the performance that will measure up in terms of the criterion rather than in terms of more important purposes. Since managers respond to the measures management actually takes to reward performance, mere verbal exhortations to behave in the manner required by long-range strategy carry no weight, and cannot be relied upon to preclude undesirable actions encouraged by a poorly designed measurement and reward system.

Faith in the efficacy of a standard measure like return on investment can reach extreme proportions, especially among managers to whom the idea of strategy is apparently unfamiliar. Instances in which performance is measured in terms of just one figure or ratio are so numerous as to suggest that the pursuit of quantification and measurement as such has overshadowed the real goal of management evaluation. If we return to our original hypothesis that profit and return on investment are terms that can be usefully employed to denote the results to be sought by business, but are too general to characterize its distinctive mission or purpose, then we must say that *short-term profitability is not by itself an adequate measure of managerial performance.* Return on investment, when used alone, is another dangerous criterion, since it can lead businessmen to postpone needed product research or the modernization of facilities in the interest of keeping down the investment on the basis of which their performance is measured. Certainly we must conclude that evaluation of performance must not be focused exclusively upon the criterion of short-run profitability or any other single standard which may cause managers to act contrary to the long-range interests of the company as a whole.

Need for multiple criteria

As you take a new look at the evaluation systems in which you are enmeshed, you will be concerned with developing better criteria. Our concern for strategy naturally leads us to suggest that the management evaluation system that plays so great a part in influencing management performance must employ a number of criteria, some of which are subjective and thus difficult to quantify. It is easy to argue that subjective judgments are unfair. But use of a harmful or irrelevant criterion just because it lends itself to quantification is a poor exchange for alleged objectivity.

Against multiple criteria, it may be argued that they restrict the freedom of the profit-center manager to produce the results required through any means he elects. This may of course be true, but the manager who does not want his methods to be subject to scrutiny does not want to be judged. Accountants, sometimes indifferent to the imperfections of their figures and the artificiality of their conventions, do not always make clear the true meaning of an annual profit figure or the extent to which a sharp rise from one year to the next may reflect a decision not to make investments needed to sustain the future of a product line.

If multiple criteria are to be used, it is not enough for top management simply to announce that short-term profitability and return on investment are only two measures among many—including responsibility to society—by which executives are going to be judged. To give subordinates freedom to exercise judgment and simultaneously to demand profitability produce an enormous pressure which cannot be effectively controlled by endless talk about tying rewards to factors other than profit.

The tragic predicament of people who, though upright in other ways, engage in bribery, "questionable payments," price fixing, and subtler forms of corruption and of their superiors who are often unaware of these practices, should dramatize one serious flaw of the profit center form of organization. Characteristically management expects this format to solve the problems of evaluation by decentralizing freedom of decision to subordinates so long as profit objectives are met. Decentralization seems sometimes to serve as a cloak for nonsupervision, except for the control implicit in the superficial measure of profitability. It would appear to preclude accurate evaluation, and the use of multiple criteria may indeed make a full measure of decentralization inappropriate.

Effective evaluation of performance

To delegate authority to profit centers and to base evaluation upon proper performance must not mean that the profit center's strategic decisions are left unsupervised. *Even under decentralization, top management must remain familiar with divisional substrategy, with the fortunes—good and bad—that attend implementation, and with the problems involved in attempting to achieve budgeted performance.* The true function of measurement is to increase perceptions of the problems limiting achievement. If an individual sees where he stands in meeting a schedule, he may be led to inquire why he is not somewhere else. If this kind of question is not asked, the answer is not proffered. An effective system of evaluation must include information which will allow top management to understand the problems faced by subordinates in achieving the results for which they are held responsible. And certainly if evaluation is to be comprehensive enough to avoid the distortions cited thus far, immediate results will not be the only object of evaluation. The effectiveness with which problems are handled along the way will be evaluated, even though this judgment, like most of the important decisions of management, must remain subjective.

The process of formulating and implementing strategy, which may be supervised directly by the chief executive in a single-unit company, can be shared widely in a multiunit company. It can be the theme of the information exchanged between organization levels. Preoccupation with final results need not be so exclusive as to prevent top management from working with divisional management in establishing objectives and policies or in formulating plans to meet objectives. Such joint endeavor helps to ensure that divisional performance will not be evaluated without full knowledge of the problems encountered in implementation.

When the diversified company becomes so large that this process is impracticable, then new means must be devised. *Implicit in accurate evaluation is familiarity with performance on a basis other than accounting figures.*

The division of corporate strategy into substrategies appropriate to each organization unit makes possible a meaningful "management by objectives" program. As superior and subordinate agree to the achievements which the subordinate will try to accomplish during the forthcoming year, priorities are dictated by strategy. The selection of objectives can be checked for the contribution they will make to the larger strategy of which they must be a part. The opportunity to discuss the relevance of a conventional objective to the total purpose of the effort undertaken can be valuable in reconciling strategy and motivation. Quantitatively unmeasureable tasks, as well as budget items, can be included in the individual's own program of action. The concept of strategy encompassing the grand purposes of the entire firm can be brought down through each discussion to a limited strategy to guide and permit evaluation of individual effort.

A shared interest in the problems to be overcome in successfully implementing individual strategy makes possible a kind of communication, an accuracy of evaluation, and a constructive influence on behavior that cannot be approached by application of a single criterion. For one manager as for a whole company, the quality of objective and of subsequent attempts to overcome obstacles posed by circumstance and by competition is the most important aspect of a manager's performance to be evaluated.

MOTIVATION AND INCENTIVE SYSTEMS

The influences upon behavior in any organization are visible and invisible, planned and unplanned, formal and not formal. The intent to measure affects the performance which is the object of measurement; cause and effect obscure each other. The executive who refuses to leave the implementation of strategy to chance has available diverse means of encouraging behavior that advances strategy and deterring behavior that does not. The positive elements, always organized in patterns that make them influential in given situations, may be designated as motivation and incentive systems. The negative elements, similarly patterned, can be grouped as systems of restraint and control. Organization studies have led their authors variously to prefer positive or negative signals and to conclude that one or the other is preferable. The general manager will do well to conclude that each is indispensable.

Executive compensation

Whatever the necessity for and the difficulties of performance evaluation, the effort to encourage and reward takes precedence over the effort to deter and restrain. Thus, properly directed, incentives may have more positive effects than control. Certainly, general manager-strategists, whose own prior experiences are likely to have made them intensely interested in the subject of executive compensation, should welcome whatever guidance they can get from researchers or staff assistants working in the field of job evaluation and compensation. Unfortunately, here also the prevailing thinking is often oriented less toward the goals to be sought than toward the requirements of the systems adopted.

Executives, like workers, are influenced by nonmonetary as well as financial incentives. At the same time, financial rewards are very important, and much thought has been given to equitable compensation of executives.

Unfortunately for the analyst of executive performance, it is harder to describe for executives than for operators at the machine what they do and how they spend their time.

The terminology of job descriptions is full of phrases like "has responsibility for," "maintains relationships with," and "supervises the operation of." The activities of planning, problem solving, and directing or administering are virtually invisible. And the activities of recruiting, training, and developing subordinates are hardly more concretely identifiable.

In any case, it is fallacious to assume that quality of performance is the only basis for the compensation of executives. Many other factors must be taken into account. The job itself has certain characteristics that help to determine the pay schedules. These include complexity of the work, the general education required, and the knowledge or technical training needed. Compensation also reflects the responsibility of job-incumbents for people and property, the nature and number of decisions they must make, and the effect of their activities and decision upon profits.

In addition to reflecting the quality of performance and the nature of the job, an executive's compensation must also have some logical relationship to rewards paid to others in the same organization. That is, the compensation system must reflect in some way a person's position in the hierarchy. On any one ladder there must be suitable steps between levels from top to bottom, if incentive is to be provided and increased scope recognized. At the same time, adjustments must be made to reflect the varying contributions that can be expected from individuals in the hierarchy of the staff versus that of the line.

Furthermore, in a compensation system, factors pertaining to the individual are almost as important as those pertaining to performance, the job, or the structure of the organization. People's age and length of service, the state of their health, some notion of their future potential, some idea of their material needs, and some insight into their views about all of these should influence either the amount of total pay or the distribution of total pay among base salary, bonuses, stock options, and other incentive measures.

Besides the many factors already listed, still another set of influences—this time coming from the environment—ordinarily affects the level of executive compensation. Included here are regional differences in the cost of living, the increments allowed for overseas assignment, the market price of given qualifications and experience, the level of local taxation, the desire for tax avoidance or delay, and the effect of high business salaries on other professions.

Just as multiple criteria are appropriate for the evaluation of performance, so many considerations must be taken into account in the compensation of executives. The company which says it pays only for results does not know what it is doing.[1]

Role of incentive pay

In addition to the problem of deciding what factors to reward, there is the equally complex issue of deciding what forms compensation should take. We would emphasize that financial rewards are especially important in business, and no matter how great the enthusiasm of people for their work, attention to the level of executive salary is an important ingredient in the achievement of strategy. Even after the desired standard of living is attained, money is still an effective incentive. Businessmen

---

[1] See Malcolm S. Salter and K. R. Sririvasa Murthy, "Should CEO Pay Be Linked to Results?" *Harvard Business Review*, May–June 1975, pp. 66–73.

used to the struggle for profit find satisfaction in their own growing net worth.

There is no question about the desirability of paying high salaries for work of great value. Yet until recently, it was clearly social policy in the United States, as elsewhere, that executive take-home pay be kept at a modest ceiling. As a consequence, profit sharing executive bonuses, stock options, performance shares, stock purchase plans, deferred compensation contracts, pensions, insurance, savings plans, and other fringe benefits have multiplied enormously. They have been directed to avoid high taxes on current income. The development of this dubious complexity has continued despite the legislation of a national earned-income tax ceiling of 50 percent. It is as incentives, however, that these various devices should be judged. Regarded as incentives to reward *individual* performance, many of these devices encounter two immediate objections, quite aside from the ethics of their tax-avoidance features. First, how compatible are the assumptions back of such rewards with the aspirations of the businessman to be viewed as a professional person? The student who begins to think of business as a profession will wonder what kind of executive will perform better with a profit sharing bonus than with an equivalent salary. We may ask whether doctors should be paid according to the longevity of their patients and whether surgeons would try harder if given a bonus when their patients survived an operation. Second, how feasible is it to distinguish any one individual's contribution to the total accomplishment of the company? And even if contribution could be distinguished and correctly measured, what about the implications of the fact that the funds available for added incentive payments are a function of total rather than of individual performance? In view of these considerations, it can at least be argued that incentives for individual performance reflect doubtful assumptions.

If, then, incentives are ruled out as an inappropriate or impractical means of rewarding individual effort, should they be cast out altogether? We believe not. There is certainly some merit in giving stock options or performance shares to the group of executives most responsible for strategy decisions, if the purpose is to assure reward for attention to the middle and longer run future.[2] There is some rationale for giving the same group current or even deferred bonuses, the amount of which is tied to annual profit, if the purpose is to motivate better cost control— something surprisingly difficult to do in a business environment marked by inflation, booming sales, and high income taxes. Certainly, too, incentive payments to the key executive group must be condoned where needed to attract and hold the scarce managerial talent without which any strategy will suffer.

In any case, as you examine the effort made by your own company to provide adequate rewards, to stimulate effective executive performance, and to inspire commitment to organizational purposes, you will wish to look closely at the relation between the incentive offered and the kind of performance needed. This observation holds as true, of course, for nonmonetary as it does for financial rewards.

Nonmonetary incentives

The area of nonmonetary incentive systems is even

[2] G. H. Foote, "Performance Shares Revitalize Stock Plans," Harvard Business Review, November–December 1973, pp. 121–30.

more difficult to traverse quickly than that of financial incentives. Executives, as human as other employees, are as much affected as anyone else by pride in accomplishment, the climate for free expression, pleasure in able and honest associates, and satisfaction in work worth doing.

They may be moved also by status symbols like office carpets, thermos sets, or office location and size. The trappings of rank and small symbols of authority are too widely cultivated to be regarded as unimportant, but little is known of their real influence. If individual contribution to organized effort is abundantly clear, little attention is likely to be given to status symbols. For example, the R&D executive with the greatest contributions to the product line may favor the "reverse status symbol" of the lab technician's cotton jacket. This is not to say that symbols have no potentially useful role to play. Office decor, for example, can be used to symbolize strategy, as when a company introduces abstract art into its central office to help dramatize its break with the past.

Very little systematic work has been done to determine what incentives or company climate might be most conducive to executive creativity, executive commitment to forward planning, executive dedication to the training of subordinates, executive striving for personal development and growth, or commitment to high standards of personal and corporate integrity. All these are of utmost value, but their impact is long-run and in part intangible. It is well known, however, that the climate most commonly extolled by managers is one where they have freedom to experiment and apply their own ideas without unnecessary constraints. Given clear objectives and a broad consensus, then latitude can be safely granted to executives to choose their own course—so long as they do not conceal the problems they encounter. In other words, executives can be presumed to respond to the conditions likely to encourage the goal-oriented behavior expected of them.

We may not always know the influence exerted by evaluation, compensation, and advancement, but if we keep purpose clear and incentive systems simple, we may keep unintended distractions to a minimum. Above all, we should be able to see the relevance to desired outcomes of the rewards offered. The harder it is to relate achievement to motives, the more cautious we should be in proposing an incentives program.

SYSTEMS OF RESTRAINT AND CONTROL

Like the system of incentives, the system of restraints and controls should be designed with the requirements of strategy in mind, rather than the niceties of complex techniques and procedures. It is the function of penalties and controls to enforce rather than to encourage—to inhibit strategically undesirable behavior rather than to create new patterns. Motivation, as we have said, is a complex of both positive and negative influences. Working in conjunction, these induce desired performance and inhibit undesirable behavior.

The need for controls—even at the executive level—is rooted in the central facts of organization itself. The inevitable consequence of divided activity is the emergence of sub-strategies, which are at least slightly deflected from the true course by the needs of individuals and the concepts and procedures of specialized groups, each with its own quasi-professional precepts and ideals. We must have controls, therefore, even in healthy and competent organizations manned by people of goodwill who are aware of organization purpose.

Formal control

Like other aspects of organizational structure and processes, controls may be both formal and informal, that is,
both prescribed and emergent. Both types are needed,
and both are important. It is, however, in the nature of
things that management is more likely to give explicit attention to the formal controls that it has itself prescribed
than to the informal controls emergent within particular
groups or subgroups.

Formal and informal controls differ in nature as well as
in their genesis. The former have to do with data that are
quantifiable, the latter with subjective values and behavior. Formal control derives from accounting; it reflects
the conventions and assumptions of that discipline and
implies the prior importance of what can be quantified
over what cannot. Its influence arises from the responsiveness of individuals—if subject to supervision and
appraisal—to information that reveals variances between
what is recorded as being expected of them and what is
recorded as being achieved. If the information depicts
variances from strategically desirable behavior, then it
tends to direct attention toward strategic goals and to
support goal-oriented policy. But if, as is more often the
case, the information simply focuses on those short-run
results which the state of the art can measure, then it di-
rects effort toward performance which, if not undesirable,
is at least biased toward short-run objectives.

To emphasize the probable shortcomings of formal or
quantifiable controls is not to assert that they have no
value. Numbers do influence behavior—especially when
pressures are applied to subordinates by superiors contemplating the same numbers. Numbers are essential in
complex organizations, since personal acquaintance with

what is being accomplished and personal surveillance over it by an owner-manager is no longer possible. As we have seen, the performance of individuals and subunits cannot be left to chance, even when acceptance and understanding of policy have been indicated and adequate competence and judgment are assured. Whether for surveillance from above or for self-control and self-guidance, numbers have a meaningful role to play, and well-selected numbers have a very meaningful role. We in no way mean to diminish the importance of figures, but only to emphasize that figures must be supplemented by informal or social controls.

Integrating formal and social control

Just as the idea of formal control is derived from accounting, the idea of informal control is derived from the inquiries of the behavioral sciences into the nature of organizational behavior. In all functioning groups, norms develop to which individuals are responsive if not obedient. These norms constitute the accepted way of doing things; they define the limits of proper behavior, and the type of action that will meet with approval from the group. In view of the way they operate, the control we have in mind is better described as *social* rather than *informal*. It is embedded in the activities, interactions, and sentiments characterizing group behavior. Sentiments take the form of likes and dislikes among people and evaluative judgments exercised upon each other. Negative sentiments, of great importance to their objects, may be activated by individual departure from a norm; such sentiments can either constitute a punishment in themselves, or can lead to some other form of punishment.

The shortcomings of formal control based on quantitative measurements of performance can be largely obviated by designing and implementing a system in which
formal and social controls are integrated. For example,
meetings of groups of managers to discuss control reports
can facilitate inquiry into the significance of problems
lying behind variances, can widen the range of solutions
considered, and can bring pressure to bear from peers as
well as from superiors. All these features can in turn contribute to finding a new course of action which addresses
the problem rather than the figures.

Enforcing ethical standards

One of the most vexing problems in attempting to establish a functional system of formal and social controls
lies in the area of ethical standards. In difficult competitive situations, the pressure for results can lead individuals into illegal and unethical practices. Instead of coun-
tering this tendency, group norms may encourage yield-
ing to these pressures. For example, knowing that others
were doing the same thing undoubtedly influenced
foreign representatives of several aircraft companies to
bribe government officials to secure contracts. Recurring
violations of price-fixing regulations, in industries beset
by overcapacity and aggressive competition, are sometimes responses to pressures to meet sales and profit expectations of a distant home office. On a lesser scale
group norms can be supportive of suppliers making expensive gifts to purchasing agents, or to sales representatives offering extravagant entertainment to customers.
The post-Watergate climate of the middle and late 1970s
has modified sharply the general attitude toward long-
established dubious practices.

When top management refuses to condone pursuit of company goals by unethical methods, it must resort to penalties like dismissal that are severe enough to dramatize its opposition. If a division sales manager, who is caught having arranged call-girl attentions for an important customer, against both the standards of expected behavior and the policy of the company, is not penalized at all, or only mildly, because of the volume of his sales and the profit he generates, ethical standards will not long be of great importance. If he is fired, then his successor is likely to think twice about the means he employs to achieve the organizational purposes that are assigned to him. When, as happened in mid-1977, a regional vice president of a large insurance firm was fired for misappropriating $250,000 of expense money, but was retained as a consultant because he controlled several millions of revenue, mixed signals are given which may confuse the communication but call attention to the dilemmas of enforcement. In due course the Internal Revenue Service may add an unambiguous comment on this transaction.

But there are limits to the effectiveness of punishment, in companies as well as in families and in society. If violations are not detected, the fear of punishment tends to weaken. A system of inspection is therefore implicit in formal control. But besides its expense and complexity, such policing of behavior has the drawback of adversely affecting the attitudes of people toward their organizations. Their commitment to creative accomplishment is likely to be shaken, especially if they are the kind of persons who are not likely to cut corners in the performance of their duties. To undermine the motivation of the ethically inclined is a high price to pay for detection of the weak. It is the special task of the Internal Audit function and the Audit Committee of the corporate board of directors not only to make investigation more effective but to

minimize its negative police-state connotations and distortions.

The student of general management is thus confronted
by a dilemma: if an organization is sufficiently decentralized to permit individuals to develop new solutions to
problems and new avenues to corporate achievement,
then the opportunity for wrongdoing cannot be elimi-
nated. This being so, a system of controls must be
supplemented by a selective system of executive recruitment and training. No system of control, no program of
rewards and penalties, no procedures of measuring and
evaluating performance can take the place of the individual who has a clear idea of right and wrong, a consistent
personal policy, and the strength to stand the gaff when
results suffer because he or she stands firm. This kind of
person is different from the human animal who grasps at
every proferred reward and flinches at every punishment.
His or her development is greatly assisted by the systems,
standards, rewards, incentives, penalties, and controls
which permit the application of qualitative criteria and
avoid the oversimplification of numerical measures. It is
always the way systems are administered that determines
their ultimate usefulness and impact.

RECRUITMENT AND DEVELOPMENT
OF MANAGEMENT

Organizational behavior, in the view we have just
taken of it, is the product of interacting *systems* of measures, motives, standards, incentives, rewards, penalties,
and controls. Put another way, behavior is the outcome of
processes of measurement, evaluation, motivation, and
control. These systems and processes affect and shape the

development of all individuals, most crucially those in management positions. Management development is therefore an ongoing process in all organizations, whether planned or not. It is appropriate however, to inquire into the need to plan this development, rather than to let it occur as it will.

In days gone by, before it was generally realized that relying on a consciously designated corporate strategy was far safer and more productive than simply trusting to good luck, a widely shared set of assumptions operated to inhibit the emergence of management development programs. These assumptions, which include the implication that managers are all male, have been described as follows:

1. Good management is instinct in action. A number of men are born with the qualities of energy, shrewdness of judgment, ambition, and capacity for responsibility. These men become the leaders of business.

2. A man prepares himself for advancement by performing well in his present job. The man who does best in competition with his fellows is best qualified to lead them.

3. If an organization does not happen to have adequate numbers of men with innate qualities of leadership who are equal to higher responsibilities, it may bring in such persons from other companies.

4. Men with the proper amount of ambition do not need to be "motivated" to demonstrate the personal qualities which qualify them for advancement.

5. Management cannot be taught formally—in school or anywhere else.[3]

---

[3]K. R. Andrews, *The Effectiveness of University Management Development Programs* (Boston: Division of Research, the Harvard Graduate School of Business Administration, 1966), p. 232.

The ideas that we have been examining here suggest that these assumptions are obsolete. People are, of course, born with different innate characteristics, but none of these precludes acquiring knowledge, attitudes, and skills which fill the gap between an identifiable personality trait and executive action. Good performance in lesser jobs is expected of persons considered for bigger jobs, but different and additional qualifications are required for higher responsiblity. Thus the most scholarly professor, the most dexterous machine operator, and the most persuasive sales representative do not necessarily make a good college president, foreman, and sales manager. The abilities that make the difference can be learned from experience or to some extent from formal education. As a substitute for training and supplying the requisite experience internally, companies can import managers trained by competitors, but this approach, though sometimes unavoidable, is risky and expensive. The risk lies in the relative difficulty of appraising the quality of outsiders and estimating their ability to transfer their technical effectiveness to a new organization. The cost lies chiefly in the disruption of natural internal incentive systems.

The supply of men and women who, of their own volition, can or will arrange for their own development is smaller than required. Advances in technology, the internationalization of markets, and the progress of research on information processing and organizational behavior all make it absurd to suppose that persons can learn all they will need to know from what they are currently doing. In particular, the activities of the general manager differ so much in kind from those of other management that special preparation for the top job should be considered, unless it is demonstrably impossible.

The success of company-sponsored and university

management training programs is evidence that the old idea that managers are born not made has been displaced by the proposition that managers are born with capacities which can be developed. In the process of seeing to it that the company is adequately manned to implement its strategy, we can identify training requirements. In other words, strategy can be our guide to (1) the skills which will be required to perform the critical tasks; (2) the number of persons with specific skill, age, and experience characteristics who will be required in the light of planned growth and predicted attrition; and (3) the number of new individuals of requisite potential who must be recruited to ensure the availability, at the appropriate time, of skills that require years to develop.

Advanced recruitment

No matter what the outcome of these calculations, it can safely be said that every organization must actively recruit new talent if it aims to maintain its position and to grow. These recruits should have adequate ability not only for filling the junior positions to which they are initially called, but also for learning the management skills needed to advance to higher positions. Like planning of all kinds, recruiting must be done well ahead of actual need.

Men and women with the ultimate capacity to become general managers should be sought out in their 20s, for able people today in a society in which the level of education as well as economic means is rising rapidly are looking more for careers than jobs. Companies should recruit—not meeting the needs for specific skills alone but making an investment in the caliber of executives who in 25 years will be overseeing activities not even contemplated at the time of their joining the company.

One of the principal impediments to effective execution of plans is shortage of management manpower of the breadth required at the time required. This shortage is the result of faulty planning, not of a natural scarcity of good raw material. Consider the bank that wishes to open 50 branches overseas as part of its international expansion. It will not be able to export and replace 50 branch managers unless, years earlier, deliberate attention has been given to securing and to training banker-administrators. These are not technicians who know only credit, for example; they must know how to preside over an entire if small bank, learn and speak a foreign language, establish and maintain relationships with a foreign government, and provide banking services not for an exclusively American but for a different group of individual and corporate customers.

After successful recruitment of candidates with high potential, speeding the course of management development is usually the only way to keep manpower planning in phase with the requirements of strategy. Thus the recruit should be put to work at a job which uses the abilities he has and challenges him to acquire the knowledge he lacks about the company and industry.

The labor force requirements imposed by commitment to a strategy of growth mean quite simply that men and women overqualified for conventional beginning assignments must be sought out and carefully cultivated thereafter. Individuals who respond well to the opportunities devised for them should be assigned to establish organization positions and given responsibility as fast as capacity to absorb it is indicated. To promote rapidly is not the point so much as to maintain the initial momentum and to provide work to highly qualified individuals that is both essential and challenging.

Continuing education

The rise of professional business education and the develoment of advanced management programs make formal training available to men and women not only at the beginning of their careers but also at appropriate intervals thereafter. Short courses for executives are almost always stimulating and often of permanent value. But management development as such is predominantly an organizational process which must be supported, not thwarted, by the incentive and control systems to which we have already alluded. Distribution of rewards and penalties will effectively determine how much attention executives will give to the training of their subordinates. No amount of lip service will take the place of action in establishing effective management development as an important management activity. To evaluate managers in part on their effort and effectiveness in bringing along their juniors requires subjective measures and a time span longer than one fiscal year. These limitations do not seriously impede judgment, especially when both strategy and the urgency of its implications for manpower development are clearly known.

In designing on-the-job training, a focus on strategy makes possible a substantial economy of effort, in that management development and management evaluation can be carried on together. The evaluation of performance can be simultaneously administered as an instrument of development. For example, any manager could use a conference with his superiors not only to discuss variances from budgeted departmental performance, but also to discover how far his or her suggested solutions are appropriate or inappropriate and why. In all such cases, discussion of objectives proposed, problems encountered, and results obtained provide opportunities for inquiry, for instruction and counsel, for learning what needs to be done and at what level of effectiveness.

Besides providing an ideal opportunity for learning, concentration on objectives permits delegation to juniors of choice of means and other decision-making responsibilities otherwise hard to come by. Throughout the top levels of the corporation, if senior management is spending adequate time on the surveillance of the environment and on the study of strategic alternatives, then the responsibility for day-to-day operations must necessarily be delegated. Since juniors cannot learn how to bear responsibility without having it, this necessity is of itself conducive to learning. If, within limits, responsibility for the choice of means to obtain objectives is also delegated, opportunity is presented for innovation, experimentation, and creative approaches to problem solving. Where ends rather than means are the object of attention and agreement exists on what ends are and should be, means may be allowed to vary at the discretion of the developing junior manager. The clearer the company's goals, the smaller the emphasis that must be placed on uniformity, and the greater the opportunity for initiative. Freedom to make mistakes and achieve success is more productive in developing executive skills than practice in following detailed how-to-do-it instructions designed by superiors or staff specialists. Commitment to purpose rather than to procedures appears to energize initiative.

Management development and corporate purpose

A stress on purpose rather than on procedures suggests that organizational climate, though intangible, is more important to individual growth than the mechanisms of personnel administration. The development of each individual in the direction best suited both to his or her own powers and to organizational needs is most likely to take place in the company where everybody is encouraged to work at the height of his or her ability and is rewarded for doing so. Such a company must have a clear idea of what it is and what it intends to become. With this idea sufficiently institutionalized so that organization members grow committed to it, the effort required for achievement will be forthcoming without elaborate incentives and coercive controls. Purpose, especially if considered worth accomplishing, is the most powerful incentive to accomplishment. If goals are not set high enough, they must be reset—as high as developing creativity and accelerating momentum suggest.

In short, from the point of view of general management, management development is not a combination of staff activities and formal training designed to provide neophytes with a common body of knowledge, or to produce a generalized good manager. Rather, development is inextricably linked to organizational purpose, which shapes to its own requirements the kind, rate, and amount of development which takes place. It is a process by which men and women are professionally equipped to be—as far as possible in advance of the need—what the evolving strategy of the firm requires them to be, at the required level of excellence.

Chief executives will have a special interest of their own in the process of management development. For standards of performance, measures for accurate evaluation, incentives, and controls will have a lower priority in their eyes than a committed organization, manned by people who know what they are supposed to do and committed to the overall ends to which their particular activities contribute. Senior managers are not blind to the needs of their subordinates to serve their own purposes as well as those of the organization. Wherever conflicting claims are made upon their attention, they require that reconciliation be found that does not obscure organizational objectives or slow down the action being taken to attain them.

Chapter eight

Strategic management and corporate governance

We have now quite carefully explored the concepts and subconcepts essential to the conscious formulation and implementation of a strategy governing the planned development of a total organization. It becomes appropriate at this point to return to the view of corporate strategy not as a concept complete and static but as an organizational process forever in motion, never ending. The merger of the process and substantive content of the concept of strategy will take us to the principal problems of corporate governance and the responsibilities of the board of directors.

STRATEGY AS A PROCESS

For the purposes of analysis, as you have already noted, we have presented strategy formulation as being reasonably complete before implementation begins, as if it made sense to know where we are going before we start. Yet we know that we often move without knowing where we will end up; the determination of purpose is in reality in dynamic interrelation with its implementation. Implementation is itself a complex process including many subprocesses of thought and organization which introduce tentativeness and doubt into prior resolution and lead us to change direction.

That strategy formulation is itself a *process of organization*, rather than the masterly conception of a single mind, must finally become clear. I made this suggestion when we were considering organization design. Many

162

facts of life conspire to complicate the simple notion that persons or organizations should decide what they can, want, and should do and then do it. The sheer difficulty of recognizing and reconciling uncertain environmental opportunity, unclear corporate capabilities and limited resources, submerged personal values, and emerging aspirations to social responsibility suggests that at least in complicated organizations strategy must be an organizational achievement and may often be unfinished. Important as leadership is, the range of strategic alternatives which must be considered in a decentralized or diversified company exceeds what one person can conceive of. As technology develops, chief executives cannot usually maintain their own technical knowledge at the level necessary for accurate personal critical discriminations. As a firm extends its activities internationally, the senior executive in the company cannot personally learn in detail the cultural and geographical conditions which require local adaptation of both ends and means.

As in all administrative processes, managing the process becomes a function distinct from performing it. The principal strategists of technically or otherwise complex organizations manage a strategic decision-making process rather than make strategic decisions. When they "make" a decision approving proposals originating from appraisals of need and opportunity made by others, they are ratifying decisions emerging from lower echelons in which the earliest and most junior participants may have played importantly decisive roles.[1] The structure of the organization, as observed earlier, may predetermine the nature of subsequent changes in strategy. In this sense

---

[1] See Joseph L. Bower, *Managing the Resource Allocation Process* (Boston: Division of Research, Harvard Business School, 1970).

strategy formulation is an activity widely shared in the hierarchy of management, rather than being concentrated at its highest levels.

Participation in strategy formulation may begin with the market manager who sees a new product opportunity or the analyst who first arranges the assumptions that make possible a 30 percent return on investment in a new venture. (A return on investment hurdle may in itself contribute to a distortion of strategy by becoming illusory goal rather than achieved result.) Because of the response to reward and punishment systems considered earlier, the strategic alternatives generated in autonomous corporate units may be the product of competition for limited resources or of divisional empire-building.

The strategy process, with its evolutionary, structural, analytical, and emotional components, encounters then the real life challenges for which conscious professional management has been devised. Opportunism remains the principal counter force; it need not be put down, for it can be turned to use. In the course of an established strategy, changing only imperceptibly in response to changing capabilities and changing market environments, sudden opportunity or major tactical decision may intrude to distract attention from distant goals to immediate gain. Thus the opportunity for a computer firm to merge with a large finance company may seem too good to pass up, but the strategy of the company will change with the acquisition or its ability to implement its strategy will be affected. A strategy may suddenly be rationalized to mean something very different from what was originally intended because of the opportunism which at the beginning of this book we declared the conceptual enemy of strategy. The necessity to accommodate unexpected opportunity in the course of continuous strategic decision is a crucial aspect of process. Accepting or refusing specific opportunity will strengthen or weaken the capability of an organization and thus alter what is probably the most crucial determinant of strategy in an organization with already developed market power.

MANAGING THE PROCESS

It is clear then that the strategic process should not be left untended. The first step is acceptance as the basis for management action of the need for a continuous process of strategic decision. This process extends from the origin of a discrete decision to its successful completion and incorporation into subsequent decisions. With this need established in an organization, the next step is to initiate the process and secure the participation first of those in senior management positions and then of those in intermediate and junior positions. The simplest way for the chief executive of a company to begin is to put corporate objectives on the agenda of appropriate meetings of functional staff, management, or directors.

Consider, for example, a large, long-established, diversified, and increasingly unprofitable company in an old industry. Its principal division was fully integrated from ownership of sources of raw materials to delivery of manufactured products to the consumer. Its president, after a day's discussion of the concept of strategy, asked his seven vice presidents, who had worked together for years, to submit to him a one-page statement expressing each officer's concept of the company's business, a summary statement of its strategy. He had in mind to go on from there, as users of this book must do. After identifying the strategy deducible from the company's established opera-

tions and taking advantage of their participation in resource allocation decisions, the president would then ask
the vice presidents to evaluate the apparent current
strategy and make suggestions for its change and improvement. This first effort to establish a conscious process of strategic decision came to a quick recess when the
president found that it took weeks to get the statements
submitted and that, once collected, they read like descriptions of seven different companies.

When discussion of current strategy resumed, a
number of key issues emerged from a study of a central
question—why so successful a company was seeing its
margins shrink and its profits decline. The communication of similar issues to those assigned responsibility to
deal with the functions they affect was an obvious next
step. The soundness of the company's recent diversification was assigned as a question to the division managers
concerned. They found themselves asked to present a
strategy for a scheduled achievement of adequate return
or of orderly divestment. The alternative uses of the company's enormous resources of raw material were examined
for the first time. The record of the research and development department, venerable in the industry for former achievements, was suddenly seen to be of little consequence in the competition that had grown up to take
away market share. Decisions long since postponed or ignored began to seem urgent. Two divisions were discontinued and expectations of improved performance began
to alter the attention of division and functional managers
throughout the organization to strategic issues.

Getting people who know the business to identify issues needing resolution, communicating these issues to
all the managers affected, and programming action leading to resolution usually lead to the articulation of a

strategy to which annual operating plans—otherwise merely numerical extrapolations of hope applied to past experience—can be successively related. It is not our purpose here, however, to present a master design for formal planning systems. This is a specialty of its own, which, like all other such specialties, needs to be related to corporate strategy but not allowed to smother or substitute for it.

When formal plans are prepared and submitted as the program to which performance is compared as a basis for evaluation, managers in intermediate position are necessarily involved in initiating projects within a concept of strategy rather than proceeding ad hoc from situation to situation. Senior managers can be guided in their approval of investment decisions by a pattern more rational than their hunches, their instinct for risk, and their faith in the track record of those making proposals, important as all these are. They have a key question to ask: what impact upon present and projected strategy will this decision make?

Sustaining the strategic process requires monitoring resource allocation with awareness of its strategic—as well as operational—consequences and its social, political, as well as financial, characteristics. Seeing to it that the process works right means that the roles of the middle-level general manager be known and appropriately supported.

As Hugo Uyterhoeven has pointed out, middle-level general managers occupy a role quite different from that of the senior general manager, relevant as is their experience as preparation for later advancement.[2] With strategic

---

[2]See Hugo F. R. Uyterhoeven, "General Managers in the Middle," *Harvard Business Review*, March–April 1972, pp. 75–85.

language and summary corporate goals coming to them from their superiors and the language and problems of everyday operations coming to them from their subordinates, they have the responsibility of translating the operational proposals, improvisations, and piecemeal solutions of their subordinates into the strategic pattern suggested to them by their superiors.

Faced with the need to make reconciliation between short-term and long-term considerations, they must examine proposals and supervise operations with an eye to their effect on long-term development. As they transform general strategic directions into operating plans and programs, they are required to practice the overview of the general manager. Their responsibility for balanced attention to short- and long-term needs and for bringing diverse everyday activities within the stream of evolving strategy far outruns their authority to require either change in strategy or to alter radically the product line of their division.

General managers at middle level, certainly in a crucial position to implement strategy in such a way as to advance it rather than depart from it, need to be protected against such distractions as performance evaluation systems overemphasizing short-term performance and to be supported continually in their duty of securing results which run beyond their authority to order certain outcomes. They need to learn how to interpret the signals they get as proposals they submit for top-management approval are accepted or turned down. Their superiors will be dependent upon their judgment as their proposals for new investment come in. Their superiors will often also be guided more by past performance or the desire to assign greater responsibility than by the detailed content of their proposals. Their seniors will do well then to realize the complexity of their juniors' position and the necessity of their being equal to the exigencies of making tactical reality subject to strategic guidance and to directing observation of operations toward appropriate amendment of strategy.

Developing the accuracy of strategic decision in a multiproduct, technically complex company requires ultimately direct attention to organization climate and individual development. The judgment required is to conduct operations against a demanding operating plan and to plan simultaneously for a changing future, to negotiate with superiors and subordinates the level of expected performance and to see, in short, the strategic implications of what is happening in the company and in its environment. The capacity of the general manager, outlined early in this book, must as part of the process of managing the strategy process be consciously cultivated, if the firm is to mature in its capacity to conduct its business and in the ability to recognize in time the changes in strategy it must effect.

Executive development, viewed from the perspective of the general manager, is essentially the nurturing of the generalist capabilities referred to throughout this book. The management of the process of strategic decision must be concerned principally with continuous surveillance of the environment and development of the internal capabilities and distinctive competence of the company. The breadth of vision and the quality of judgment brought to the application of corporate capability to environmental opportunity are crucial. The senior managers who keep their organization involved continuously in appraising its performance against its goals, appraising its goals against the company's concept of its place in its industry and in society, and debating openly and often the continued validity of its strategy will find corporate attention to strategic questions gradually proving effective in letting the organization know what it is, what its activities are about, where it is going, and why its existence and growth are worth the best contributions of its members.

The chief executive of a company has as his or her highest function the management of a continuous process of strategic decision in which a succession of corporate objectives of ever-increasing appropriateness provides the means of economic contribution, the necessary commensurate return, and the opportunity for the men and women of the organization to live and develop through productive and rewarding careers.

THE STRATEGIC FUNCTION OF THE BOARD OF DIRECTORS

If the highest function of the chief executive is the management of the future-oriented purposeful development of the enterprise, then it is necessarily the responsibility of the board of directors to see that this job is adequately done. Although in the common conception of corporate governance the board is ultimately responsible, its outside directors cannot themselves customarily originate the strategy they must approve. The chief recourse of directors ratifying strategy in highly complex situations is not to substitute their judgment for that of management but to see that the proposals presented to them have been properly prepared and can be defended as strategically consistent and superior to available alternatives. If they are flawed they are usually withdrawn for revision by management. Although the board is usually unable to originate strategy, its detachment from operations equips it to analyze developing strategic decisions with fresh objectivity and breadth of experience. It can be free of the management myopia sometimes produced by operations, in places where keeping things going obscures the direction they are taking.

Under pressure from the public, from the Securities and Exchange Commission, and indirectly from the U.S. Senate's Subcommittee on Shareholders' Rights, the board of directors is undergoing revitalization as the only available source of legitimacy for corporate power and assurance of corporate responsibility, given the archaism of corporation law and the dispersed ownership of the large public corporation.

The consensus developing in the current revival of board effectiveness is that working boards will not only actively support, advise, and assist management but also will monitor and evaluate management's performance in the attainment of planned objectives. Boards nowadays are expected to exhibit in decision behavior their responsibility (while representing the economic interest of the shareholders) for the legality, integrity, and ethical quality of the corporation's activities and financial reporting, and their sensitivity to the interests of segments of society legitimately concerned about corporate performance.

For our purposes here the central function of a working board is to review the management's formulation and implementation of strategy and to exercise final authority in ratifying with good reason management's adherence to established objectives and policy or in contributing constructively to management's recommendation for change.

It is now widely recognized that boards should be diversely composed, should consist largely of outside directors, should structure themselves to make their monitoring functions practicable. All firms registered on the New York Stock Exchange must have audit committees, for example, as a condition of membership. Their functions are to recommend to the board and then to shareholders the choice of external auditors, to ensure to the extent possible that the company's control personnel are generating and reporting accurate and complete data fairly representing the financial performance of the company, and to ascertain that internal auditors are examining in detail situations in which the company is vulnerable to fraud or improper behavior.

Despite the assumptions of some regulatory agency personnel, it is of course not possible for outside directors to detect fraud or identify questionable payments with their own eyes when well-intentioned and competent management auditors have not been able to do so. Their contribution is to inquire into the quality of intention, competence, and process, to observe the capability and command of information of those reporting to the committee, and to raise questions prompted by experience not available in the company. When necessary they recommend to the board replacement of controllers or change of auditors.

Executive compensation committees are expected to oversee the incentive and salary programs of the companies and to set the compensation of the most senior managers, in the course of that activity evaluating their performance. A trend is developing toward the establishment of nominating committees to consider executive succession, board composition, and performance, and to make recommendations to the board of new members. The flow of information to these committees is supposed to economize the time and inform the judgment of the independent directors and to enable them to appraise the caliber of the company's management. The possibility of overwhelming outsiders with information is always imminent. Information usable by the board cannot usually be siphoned out of the management information systems. Organization and selection to serve the special functions of the board are required.

In view of the difficulty entailed in enabling independent directors to pass judgment on strategic decisions, it is interesting to note that among the development of other committees (like public responsibility and legal affairs) strategy committees of the board, whatever they might be called, have not come into wide use. It appears likely that as boards become aware of the need to relate approval of specific investment decisions to the purposes of the company, they may wish to focus the attention of some of the directors upon strategic questions now presented without prior detailed consideration to the full board.

Like members of the audit and compensation committees, board members assigned to give additional time to the evaluation of total strategy could in theory become familiar not necessarily with the detailed debates shaping specific strategic alternatives but with how the strategic process is managed in the company. You may wish to consider the extent to which familiarity with the strategy of your company and the ability to relate financial performance to it would affect the evaluation by the board of the chief executive officer's performance and to what extent such familiarity is available otherwise.

In most boards at present it is assumed that the independent directors will support the chief executive until it is necessary to remove him. Removal ordinarily comes late after disaster has struck or after early strategic mistakes have produced repeated irretrievable losses. The go/no-go dilemma, which does not apply in any other superior-subordinate relationship in the corporation, could presumably be replaced by discussion and debate at board level of strategic questions presented to the board by the chief executive officer. When interim remediable dissatisfaction with the quality of this discussion appeared, advice to the chief executive officer could be offered in time for it to do some good. The chief executive's longevity is extended in some situations by his securing the participation of the board in crucial strategic decisions. When one of these decisions fails after such participation, responsibility is shared by the board and the chief executive rather than borne by the latter alone. Routine ratification, without real discussion, does not secure the commitment of directors to any major decision. The attainment of board commitment is sometimes complicated by insecurity, unwillingness to share power, and lack of skill in board management on the part of the chief executive officers.

The problem of securing competent outside director preparation and participation is compounded by the relationship resulting from the simple fact that independent directors have ordinarily owed their board membership to the chairman or chief executive officer they are supposed to evaluate. It is possible that the active participation of nominating committees will increase the independence of boards, especially if the chief executive officers participating in the selection process want such a result.

The management of effective boards of directors is presently being studied. The power of strategy as a simplifying concept enabling independent directors to know the business (in a sense) without being in the business will one day be more widely tested at board level. If strategic management can be made less intuitive and more explicit, it will be possible for management directors and chief executive officers to identify existing strategy, evaluate it against the criteria we suggested at the beginning of this book, consider alternatives for improvement in the presence of the board, and make recommendations to a board equipped to make an intelligent critical response in strategic terms—that is relating specific proposals to corporate strategy. The ability to sense the pattern of progress in the welter of operations is essential to all executives and directors who do not want to get lost in the trees around them.

Strategic management comes to its culmination in the chairmanship of effective boards. For the moment, the Securities and Exchange Commission, the Department of Justice, and the Federal Trade Commission appear to prefer the restructured and revitalized board of directors as the route to a kind of corporate governance sufficiently responsible to meet current concerns about autonomous management power. Most defenders of our mixed economic system prefer this approach to the introduction of new regulation. Voluntary adaptation to public expectations allows the special circumstances of each industry and company situation to be taken into account; regulation does not. On the other hand doing nothing remains a possible response to the call for voluntary action.

The mastery of the concept of strategy makes easier the kind of discussion in board rooms that helps managements make better decisions. It performs this function by reducing the world of detail to be considered to those central aspects of external environment and internal resources that affect the company and bear on the definition of its business. The special skill involved in perceiving and communicating the strategic significance of a business decision may be of the highest importance in engaging independent directors in the exercise of their assumed responsibility and in establishing active and effective boards as normal adjuncts to competent professional management. Such a development may reduce the likelihood that corporate governance will be judged sufficiently irresponsible that radical legislative checks are imposed upon corporate freedom and initiative.

Index